A VOCABULARY WORKBOOK THRU READING

Prefixes, Roots, and Suffixes for College Students

Yi-kyun No

(주)백산출판사

머리말

First of all, my thanks should go to the Lord God and my parents. Without them, I wouldn't be here today.

I have written this book in the hope that it will stimulate and inform my students who are to prepare for Toeic, Toefl, and IELTS. If there is a bias in my selection of example sentences to cover, it is only in favor of those sentences which will be of most interest to students who want to get used to those sentences which are often quoted from those three main tests mentioned previously.

Like the ability to play the piano, ride a bike, or solve a calculus problem, the ability to analyze etymology can be acquired and refined only through practice, especially reading practice. Students need to "get their hands dirty" in the data of a wide range of vocabulary, both familiar and unfamiliar, before they can fully appreciate the principles of etymological analysis and the structure, organization, and the use of vocabulary.

This book has been created to provide such practice. I have significantly used a number of exercises, including more elementary ones and a large section of intermediate and advanced ones, too. I also have added a list of key spellings to help students better understand all the vocabulary in each exercise. I can say that the result is a reasonably balanced mixture of fact and theory, and of enthusiasm and sobriety. Besides, into this book a lot of schemata needed in such three main tests as Toeic, Toefl, and IELTS having been gathered up from my 33-year-old teaching experience has been permeated.

This book owes a great deal to my family, especially to my wife. Though in poor condition, she did more than her fair share of taking care of her family. Without the support of my spouse, this book would not be born into the world. For the love and encouragement from such my family as my wife, my daughter Sarah, and my son John, I express heartfelt thanks.

I always welcome comments on this book.

July 26, 2018

Looking at Mt. Gwanak

Yi-kyun No

차례

Chapter I Prefixes and Suffixes

I

Chapter ▸▸

Prefixes and Suffixes

1 pre
2 a[an]
3 ad
4 post
5 com
6 de
7 ex
8 in
9 pro
10 mis
11 sub
12 in
13 re
14 un
15 trans
16 ob
17 ab
18 inter
19 mono and poly
20 anti
21 syn
22 dis
23 non
24 mal

1 pre

1.1 Meaning: before

The prefix **pre** may mean before in time, before in order or rank, or before in place.

EXERCISE A Definitions of Useful pre Words

premise	His theory is based on a premise which every physics student knows.
prematurely	A prematurely born baby must receive special treatment.
prefer	Most Americans prefer coffee to tea.
preliminary	After a few preliminary remarks, Dr. Smith spoke on the problems of working mothers.
predict	Almost everyone predicts that the population of India will continue to increase.

precede An informal tea preceded the business meeting.

1.____________ To foretell an event, to tell beforehand what will happen later.

2.____________ To go, come, or be earlier than something else; to be or take place before something else

3.____________ Introductory; introducing the main business or topic of a speech

4.____________ A statement that is assumed to be true, which comes before a group of related statements that may or may not be true and can be debated and argued about

5.____________ To like something better than something else (to put something before something else, to give it first place)

6.____________ Too early, happening before the proper or usual time

1.2 Prefix or Not?

The letters *pre* at the beginning of a word may not always be the prefix **pre**. For example, the word *press* does not contain the prefix **pre**.

How can you tell whether or not the letters *pre* at the beginning of a word from the prefix **pre**?

Look at the part of the word that follows these three letters. Does this part of the word ever occur as a word by itself? For example, in the word *pretest*, the second part, *test,* is a word that can stand alone.

Another way to check whether or not the letters *pre* at the beginning of a word form the prefix **pre** is to try to substitute a different prefix. For example, in the word *prepare*, the prefix **com** can be substituted for the prefix **pre**, producing the word *compare*.

In other words, ask yourself two questions about the word part that follows the letters *pre*. Can it stand alone as a word? Can a different prefix be substituted for *pre*, producing a word? If the answer to either of these questions is yes, then you are probably dealing with the prefix **pre**.

EXERCISE B Prefix or Not?

1. **a.** prewar **b.** pretty **c.** preview **d.** present
2. **a.** premature **b.** presurvey **c.** pressure **d.** preside
3. **a.** preach **b.** prearrange **c.** preadolescent **d.** pretend
4. **a.** prebake **b.** prefer **c.** preposition **d.** prey
5. **a.** presume **b.** preheat **c.** pretzel **d.** preface
6. **a.** president **b.** preschool **c.** prefix **d.** preen

2 a[an]

2.1 Meaning: not; without, lacking; absence of

EXERCISE A Definitions of Useful a[an] Words

atypical The behavior of monkeys in a zoo is atypical; they are very different animals in their natural environment.

anarchy People's lives and property are not safe if the country is in a state of anarchy.

anonymous An anonymous letter is often the product of a sick mind.

anemic An anemic person looks pale and feels tired.

atheist Deeply religious people pity the atheist as someone who cannot turn to God for help.

apathetic The child's illness made him apathetic; he did not even look at the toys his father brought him.

1.____________ Absence of government; political disorder because there is no law or government

2.____________ Not of typical character; irregular; unlike the type

3.____________ A person who does not believe in the existence of God

4.____________ Without a signature; bearing no name; by a writer who does not declare his or her name

5.____________ Without feeling or emotion; uninterested in what usually arouses feeling or interest

6.____________ Suffering from lack of red corpuscles or hemoglobin in the blood

2.2 A Variant Form of the Prefix a: an

This prefix has two forms: **a** and **an**. Which form should be used?

The rule is like the rule for the words *a* and *an*: *a* book, *an* apple. If the word part following the prefix begins with a vowel, the letter *n* is added, and the form used is **an**. If the word part following the prefix does not begin with a vowel, the form used is **a**.

EXERCISE B a or an?

1. osmia ____________
2. theism ____________
3. septic ____________
4. aerobic ____________
5. algesia ____________
6. phonic ____________

2.3 Prefix or Not?

Many words begin with *a* or *an*, but these letters do not always form the prefix **a**[**an**].
For example, the *a* of the word *ask* is not the prefix **a**; the letters *an* that begin the word *and* do not form the prefix **an**. How can you tell when these letters form the prefix?

Look at the part of the word following the letters *a* or *an*. If this part can stand alone as a word, then you probably have the prefix **a**[**an**]. This is true in the case of a word like *atypical*, where *typical* is a word that occurs alone, without the prefix **a**.

Another way to check whether or not the letters *a* or *an* form the prefix **a**[**an**] is to try to substitute a different prefix. For example, in the word *apathetic*, the prefix **sym** can be substituted for the prefix **a**, forming the word *sympathetic.*

In other words, ask yourself two questions about the word part that follows the letters *a[an]*. Can it stand alone as a word? Can a different prefix be substituted, producing a word? If the answer to either of these questions is yes, then you may be dealing with the prefix **a**[**an**]. However, there are many exceptions. You know one of them: the word *alike*. You know another: *another*.

EXERCISE C Prefix or Not?

1. apathy ____________	6. amoral ____________
2. ape ____________	7. asexual ____________
3. anarchy ____________	8. asked ____________
4. admit ____________	9. architect ____________
5. alter ____________	10. aim ____________

3 ad

3.1 Meaning: to, toward

EXERCISE A Definitions of Useful ad Words

adjacent	When Mr. and Mrs. Smith stayed at a hotel, they took adjacent rooms for themselves and their two children.
advocate	He is an advocate of free university education for all.
assent	The director assented to the suggestion that employees of the company hold a monthly meeting.
adhere	She adheres to the highest moral principles.
aggression	Our country will strike back at those who commit an act of aggression against us.
administer	A small group of experts will administer a program to increase the production of milk.

1.____________ To agree to, to consent to

2.____________ An attack, a hostile act (towards someone)

3.____________ A supporter, someone who defends or supports a cause

4.____________ To carry out, to execute, to manage or direct

5.____________ To be devoted to, to be firmly attached to, to hold tightly to

6.____________ Neighboring; next to each other

3.2 Variant Forms of the Prefix ad

ac, af, ag, al, an, ap, ar, as, at

The prefix **ad** has more variant forms than any other prefix. In other words, it is more influenced than any other prefix by the word parts that it precedes. In the following examples, notice how the letter *d* of the prefix **ad** changes to match the first letter of the word part that is added to it.

ad	+	cept	accept
ad	+	fix	affix
ad	+	gression	aggression
ad	+	lot	allot
ad	+	notate	annotate
ad	+	pend	append
ad	+	range	arrange
ad	+	sume	assume
ad	+	tach	attach

EXERCISE B ad or Variant Forms

1. **ad** + ply ______________
2. **ad** + mit ______________
3. **ad** + cumulate ______________
4. **ad** + fection ______________
5. **ad** + apt ______________
6. **ad** + mire ______________
7. **ad** + gravate ______________
8. **ad** + vise ______________
9. **ad** + sociate ______________
10. **ad** + verb ______________

3.3 Prefix or Not?

The letters *ad* at the beginning of a word do not always mean that the prefix **ad** is present. As in the case of other prefixes, you must look at the second part of the word. Can it stand by itself as a word? If so, then the letters *ad* are probably the prefix **ad**. For example, if we remove the letters *ad* from the word *administer*, we have minister, which can stand alone as a word. Therefore, the letters *ad* must be the prefix **ad**.

Another test is to see if we can substitute another prefix. We can take the prefix **sub** and change the word *admit* to *submit*. In cases like this, we are probably dealing with the prefix **ad**.

As for the variant forms of **ad**, we must remember that the prefix **ad** changes its form because of the second part of the word, as explained in part **3.2** of this section. Therefore, if *ad*, *af*, *ag*, *al*, *an*, *ap*, *as*, or *at* at the beginning of a word are variant forms of the prefix **ad**, the consonant will always be doubled: **acc**, **aff**, **agg**, **all**, **ann**, **app**, **arr**, **ass**, **att**, as in the words *accept*, *affix*, *aggression*, *allot*, *annotate*, *append*, *arrange*, *assume*, and *attach*. If these consonants are not doubled, then the word does not contain a variant form of the prefix **ad**.

The following words, therefore, do not contain a variant form of the prefix **ad**, because the second consonant is not doubled: *action*, *aflame*, *agate*, *alien*, *anodyne*, *apiary*, *artist*, *aster*, and *athlete*.

EXERCISE C Prefix or Not?

1.	**a.** atrium	**b.** attend	**c.** attract	**d.** attest
2.	**a.** apply	**b.** appeal	**c.** apish	**d.** apposition
3.	**a.** architect	**b.** arrive	**c.** arrest	**d.** arrear
4.	**a.** assume	**b.** assure	**c.** associate	**d.** ass
5.	**a.** affirm	**b.** affect	**c.** afterward	**d.** afflict
6.	**a.** adverse	**b.** adze	**c.** advise	**d.** adjoin

4 post

4.1 Meaning: after, behind, following

EXERCISE A Definitions of Useful post Words

postscript Just as he was about to seal the envelope, he remembered that he had forgotten to mention his plans for a trip, so he took out his letter and added that information in a postscript.

posterity The rivers and trees of the world do not belong only to us; they belong to posterity.

postgraduate Susan majored in psychology at Harvard University, where she received her B.A. last year. Now she is planning to do post-graduate studies in the same field but at a different university.

postoperative	Some doctors believe that the success of an operation depends on postoperative care received by the patient.
postdate	Here's a check for the money I owe you. I won't have money in the bank to cover it until I get my salary next week, so I'll postdate the check. You'll have to wait a week to cash it.
postpone	The students asked Dr. Smith to postpone the examination.

1.____________ All generations to come; all following generations

2.____________ Sentences added after a letter or other document has been written

3.____________ To put off until a later date

4.____________ To give a date that is later than the actual date

5.____________ Related to studies that are carried out after graduation from a university

6.____________ Related to the period following surgery

4.2 Using a Hyphen with the Prefix post

Sometimes a hyphen is used between the prefix **post** and the second part of the word.

The rule is simple: If the second part of the word is a word that always begins with a capital letter, then a hyphen is used. For example, **post** and *Aztec* combine to form *post-Aztec.* But **post** and *anesthetic* combine to form *postanesthetic.*

EXERCISE B Hyphenated or Not?

1. Biblical ____________
2. natal ____________
3. classical ____________
4. Darwinian ____________
5. hypnotic ____________
6. election ____________
7. Renaissance ____________
8. nuptial ____________
9. Jurassic ____________
10. marital ____________

A VOCABULARY WORKBOOK THRU READING

REVIEW OF SECTIONS 1, 2, 3, and 4

EXERCISE A Recall of Useful Words

pre [Section 1.1]

1.______________ To foretell [---d--t]

2.______________ To go or come before [---c-d-]

3.______________ Introductory [---lim--ary]

4.______________ An assumption leading to a conclusion [---m-s-]

5.______________ To like better [---fe-]

6.______________ Early, before the proper time [---m-t-re]

a [Section 2.1]

1.______________ Without a system of government [--ar--y]

2.______________ Not expected, not usual [-typ---l]

3.______________ A person who does not believe in God [-th---t]

4.______________ Without a signature [--onym--s]

5.____________ Without feeling or interest [-path--ic]

6.____________ Suffering from lack of red blood cells [--em--]

ad [Section 3.1]

1.____________ To express agreement [--s-nt]

2.____________ An act of hostility [--gress---]

3.____________ A supporter [--vo-ate]

4.____________ To carry out [--min---er]

5.____________ To be firmly attached to [--h-r-]

6.____________ Next to each other [--ja-ent]

post [Section 4.1]

1.____________ All future generations [----er--y]

2.____________ An addition to a letter that is finished [----scr--t]

3.____________ To put off [----p--e]

4.____________ To write a date that is later than the real date [-----ate]

5.____________ Related to a program of study followed by a graduate of a university [----gr------]

6.____________ Related to the period after a medical operation [----op-----ve]

EXERCISE B Recall of Useful Words

1. __________ A person who writes __________onymous letters does not sign them.
2. It is normal to __________fer pleasure to pain.
3. Most students in __________graduate programs have made low grades as college students.
4. It is easier to __________minister a test than to write one.
5. Hitting another person is an act of __________gression.
6. Most hospitals have a special room for __________mature babies.
7. Study should __________cede the taking of an examination.
8. She added a short __________script to the letter she had written.
9. __________theists are not welcome in extremely religious communities.
10. After a few __________liminary exercises, the players started the game.
11. She will __________sent to your plan if it saves time and money.
12. Rain is __________typical weather for the desert.

13. Because of poor __________operative care, the patient died, although the surgeon had been skillful.
14. It is __________dicted that a vaccine against cancer will be developed.
15. Our generation will be hated by __________erity if we use all the oil and coal reserves of the earth.
16. A short period of __________archy followed the revolution before a dictator seized power.
17. Neighbors in __________jacent apartments are not always friends.
18. He __________heres to his father's political beliefs.
19. We cannot __________pone attempts to develop new sources of energy.
20. Although it was based on a widely accepted __________mise, his argument was weak.
21. He wrote two letters to his aunt and __________dated one of them, so that she would be-lieve he had written to her on two separate occasions.
22. The students were __________pathetic because it was very hot and also because it was the last hour of the school day.
23. He is a stronger __________vocate of women's rights than many women are.

24. An __________emic person tires easily.

EXERCISE C Using Prefix Meaning to Understand New Words

1. Babies are *amoral* creatures.
   a. They usually receive a great deal of attention.
   b. They have no sense of what is right and what is wrong.
   c. They cry a lot, but they also laugh a lot.
   d. Their development after birth is slower than before birth.

2. Mary will *preside* at tomorrow's meeting.
   a. attend, come to
   b. not attend, be absent
   c. take charge of, lead
   d. talk, make a speech

3. He *appended* a few paragraphs to the final copy of the report.
   a. added to the report
   b. removed from the report

c. declared that they were important

d. stated that they were of no importance

4. They decided to give a *postelection* party.

a. during the election

b. before the election

c. after the election

d. because of the election

5. The *preamble* to her speech was very interesting.

a. the reaction to it

b. the final part

c. the subject

d. the introduction or first part

6. The doctor advised him to take an *analgesic* medicine.

a. It caused him to feel no pain.

b. It had to be taken before meals.

c. It had to be taken after meals.

d. It was intended to make him well.

7. They had a *postmeridiem* swim every day.

a. early in the morning

b. in the afternoon

c. in the ocean

d. in fresh water

8. In 1982, the people at the club meetings were *preponderantly* men.

   a. higher in number [more men than women]

   b. lower in number [fewer men than women]

   c. seldom [men almost never attended]

   d. at the end [in the final months of 1982]

9. They took rooms in the hotel *annex.*

   a. the main part of the hotel

   b. a building attached to the hotel

   c. the top floor of the hotel

   d. a part of the hotel with no bathrooms

10. The report was *annotated.*

    a. Some comments and explanations were added to it.

    b. It was extremely important.

    c. It had no title.

    d. It was written after the busy season.

5 com

5.1 Meaning: with, together

EXERCISE A Definitions of Useful com Words

committee	Everyone on the committee worked hard, but Mary worked the hardest.
congregate	Students congregate in the cafeteria between classes.
coexist	In many countries, private business companies and government-controlled companies coexist.
collide	No one was hurt when the school bus collided with a car yesterday, because both were traveling at low speed.
correlation	Educators are not certain that there is any correlation between students' grades and the amount of time they spend studying.
convention	Every year, the teachers of every school

in the state choose dele-gates to represent them at the state teachers' convention.

1.____________ A relationship which can be measured

2.____________ A small group people who meet together regularly for some common purpose

3.____________ The coming together of a large group at a formal, organized meeting

4.____________ To gather or assemble together, often in an informal, unorganized manner

5.____________ To exist at the same time or place (to exist together)

6.____________ To strike or crash against each other (together)

co, col, con, cor

The prefix **com** has several variant forms, depending on the beginning letter of the word part that follows.

co Look at these words: coexist, coaxial, coincide, and cooperate. In each case, the prefix **com** appears as **co** before a word part that begins with a vowel. The variant form **co** also appears if the second part of the word begins with the letter h or w, as in the words cohabit and coworker.

col If the prefix **com** is used with a word part that begins with the letter l, the variant form **col** is used, as in the word collide.

con In the same way, **com** is replaced by **con** if the prefix is used with a word part that begins with one of these letters: c, d, f, g, q, s, t, or v. Examples are the words: congregate and convention.

cor When **com** is used with a word part that begins with the letter r, the vari-ant form **cor** appears, as in the word correlation.

EXERCISE B com, co, col, con, or cor?

1. **com** + education ____________
2. **com** + ference ____________
3. **com** + tend ____________
4. **com** + bine ____________
5. **com** + rect ____________
6. **com** + lusion ____________
7. **com** + extend ____________

8. **com** + here ____________

9. **com** + league ____________

10. **com** + mission ____________

11. **com** + dole ____________

12. **com** + gratulate ____________

The letters com, co, col, con, and cor at the beginning of a word may not always be the prefix **com** or one of its variant forms. The second part of the word will usually give us information on this question. If the second part of the word can stand alone as a word by itself, then we are probably dealing with a prefix. This is true of the coworker, for example. The second part, worker, occurs by itself as a word. There-fore, the letters co are the prefix **co**.

Another test is to try to substitute another prefix at the beginning. If we can do this, we are probably dealing with a prefix. For example, we can substitute **pre** for the first three letters of the word convention, producing the word prevention. Therefore, the letters con in this word are the prefix **con**.

In other words, ask yourself two questions about the word part that follows the letters com. Can it stand alone as a word? Can a different prefix be substituted, producing a word? If the answer to either of these questions is yes, then you may be dealing with the prefix **com**.

EXERCISE C Prefix or Not?

1. **a.** coauthor **b.** coast **c.** coequal **d.** coefficient
2. **a.** conch **b.** conclude **c.** concise **d.** concord
3. **a.** compound **b.** command **c.** commingle **d.** coma
4. **a.** collateral **b.** color **c.** collocate **d.** collinear
5. **a.** context **b.** cone **c.** contest **d.** contribute
6. **a.** commission **b.** compare **c.** comma **d.** compel

The prefix **con** may be confused with the prefix **contra(contro)**, meaning against, as in the word contrary. However, the meaning of words that begin with the prefix **contra(contro)** can usually be guessed from the rest of the sentence in which they appear. It is the meaning which helps students decide whether the prefix is **con** or **contra(contro)**.

EXERCISE D con or contra(contro)?

1. There is a great contrast between the desert and the green farmland at its edge. (Prefix: __________)
2. Because Tom's ideas were so different from Bob's, the two men had many contro-versies. (Prefix: __________)
3. He read the contract for a four-room apartment very care-fully before singing it. (Prefix: __________)
4. If you contravene the law, you will be punished. (Prefix: __________)

6 de

6.1 Meaning: down; from; away; off; completely

EXERCISE A Definitions of Useful de Words

depression After his wife's death, he entered a long period of depression.

derive Many words in English are derived from Greek or Latin.

denounce He was denounced for helping the enemies of his country.

deduction He made the right deduction about the identity of the killer because he had been a detective for many years.

decline Very few countries have experienced a decline in population in recent years.

devote Great achievers are often those who have devoted themselves to one field of interest.

1.____________ To condemn, to state that someone or something is evil or bad

2.____________ Unhappiness; an abnormal or unhealthy state of inactivity (being down)

3.____________ To give oneself completely to something, to give one's energy and time to something

4.____________ A reduction; a lessening or lowering (going down from large to small)

5.____________ To receive from, as something is received from a certain source or ori-gin.

6.____________ A conclusion reached by using logic or reasoning

The letters de at the beginning of a word do not always form the prefix **de**.

If the word part following the letters de can stand by itself as a word, then the prefix **de** is probably present. An example is the word demagnetize. Since magnetize is an independent word, we can assume that the letters de form the prefix **de**. But if we take the word death and remove the letters de, we are left with ath, which is not a word. Therefore, we conclude that in the word death, the letters de do not form the prefix **de**.

The second test to determine if the letters de form the prefix **de** is to see if an-other prefix can be substituted. For example, we can remove the letters de from the word reduction. If we take the word death and put the prefix **re** in place of the letters de, we have reach, which is not a word. We can try other prefixes, such as **sub**, **pre**, **com**, etc., but we cannot produce a word.

In other words, ask yourself two questions about the word part that follows the letters de. Can it stand alone as a word? Can a different prefix be substituted, producing a word? If the answer to either of these questions is yes, then you may be dealing with the prefix **de**.

EXERCISE B Prefix or Not?

1. **a.** dearth **b.** depress **c.** defer **d.** deception
2. **a.** dethrone **b.** dewy **c.** delimit **d.** depend
3. **a.** detract **b.** deceive **c.** devil **d.** derail
4. **a.** depart **b.** desk **c.** derange **d.** demote
5. **a.** delft **b.** desist **c.** denounce **d.** deplore
6. **a.** demand **b.** defile **c.** deepen **d.** deflect

7 ex

7.1 Meaning: out; from; former

EXERCISE A Definitions of Useful ex Words

emit	Almost all sources of light emit heat.
exclude	There are not many organizations in America today that exclude women.
expose	Exposing your skin to the sun may result in a healthy tan, but too much sun may cause skin cancer in some individuals.
external	His external appearance did not reveal his severe psychological problems.
extract	The pain she felt when her tooth was extracted was less severe than she had feared.
execution	The successful execution of their plan depended on an intelligent and hard-working woman.

1.____________ To remove, to take out

2.____________ To give off, to send out

3.____________ Management; the act of carrying out or performing a task or duty

4.____________ Outer, outside

5.____________ To shut out, to keep out, to refuse entrance to

6.____________ To show, to reveal (to lay out)

7.2 Variant Forms of the Prefix ex

e, ex (ec, es)

ef When the prefix **ex** is followed by a word part beginning with the letter f, the variant form **ef** is used, as in the word effect.

e The letter x is dropped from the prefix **ex**, producing the variant form **e**, when the prefix **ex** is followed by a word beginning with one of these letters: b, d, g, l, m, n, r or v. Examples are the words: evolve, elect, and emit.

(There are a few words in which the prefix **ex** becomes **ec** or **es** when the word part that follows begins with the letter c. For example, **ex** followed by the word part cape becomes **es**, as in escape. However, **ex** often remains **ex** even when followed by a word part beginning with the letter c. For example, **ex** followed by the word part cavate remains **ex**, as in excavate. Therefore, think of the variant **ec** and **es** forms as exceptions to the usual patterns.)

EXERCISE B ex, e, or ef?

1. **ex** + fect ____________
2. **ex** + mission ____________
3. **ex** + voke ____________
4. **ex** + hale ____________
5. **ex** + rupt ____________
6. **ex** + lated ____________
7. **ex** + clude ____________
8. **ex** + numerate ____________
9. **ex** + gress ____________
10. **ex** + ception ____________

The letters ex, e, or ef at the beginning of a word are not always the prefix **ex** or one of its variant forms.

As in the case of other prefixes, we must look at the word part following these letters. Can it stand alone as a word? If not, can we substitute another prefix in place of the letters ex, e, or ef and produce a word? If the answer to either of those questions is yes, then we are probably dealing with the prefix **ex** or one of its variant forms, **e** or **ef**.

EXERCISE C Prefix or Not?

1. evil ____________
2. cvincc ____________
3. evolutiom ____________
4. exact ____________
5. effluence ____________
6. egglike ____________
7. egg ____________
8. everybody ____________
9. erect ____________
10. elsewhere ____________

When the prefix **ex** is used to mean former, as in the words ex-wife and ex-consul, a hyphen usually separates it from the following word part. The variant forms of **ex(e** and **ef)** are never used in these words, no matter what letter begins the word part that follows the hyphen.

EXERCISE D Hyphenated or Not?

1. **ex** + presiden ____________
2. **ex** + cellent ____________
3. **ex** + communicate ____________
4. **ex** + vice-president ____________
5. **ex** + change ____________
6. **ex** + citement ____________
7. **ex** + ambassador ____________
8. **ex** + husband ____________

The prefix **extra** means beyond, outside of, or outside the scope of. For example, an extragovernmental problem is a problem that is not to be dealt with by the government, or a problem that does not concern the government.

It is fairly easy to avoid confusion between the prefix **ex** and **extra**. If a word begins with the letters extra, look at the part that follows. If it is a complete word, like governmental, then the prefix is **extra**.

EXERCISE E ex or extra?

1. extrajudicial ____________
2. extradite ____________
3. extraterritorial ____________
4. extraordinary ____________
5. extraparliamentary ____________
6. extraction ____________
7. extraprofessional ____________

8 in

8.1 Meaning: in, into; within

EXERCISE A Definitions of Useful in Words

imply	She implied that she was in a hurry by glancing at her watch several times.
income	His income is so small that he barely meets his expenses and can not possibly save any money.
induce	She induced her little boy to drink his milk by promising to tell him a story when he had finished it.
illustrate	To illustrate this economic principle, Dr. Smith told an amusing story.
irrigate	Farmers in areas where there is little rainfall raise crops by irrigating the land.
involve	John was involved in an attempt to rob the largest bank in town.

1.____________ To supply land with water through pipes or channels (to bring water in)

2.____________ Money earned, money from a job, a business, etc. (money that comes in)

3.____________ To hint; to express something without saying it or without saying it openly

4.____________ To make a part of' to draw in

5.____________ To persuade, to get someone to do something (to lead someone into something)

6.____________ To make something clear, especially by using figures, examples, or pictures (to put light into)

8.2 Variant Forms of the Prefix in

il, im, ir

As in the case of other prefixes with variant forms, the prefix **in** may appear as **il**, **im**, or **ir** because of the beginning letter of the word part that follows it.

il The variant form **il** is used when the following word part begins with the letter l. An example is the word illustrate.

ir The variant form **ir** is used when the following word part begins with the letter r. An example is the word irrigate.

im The variant form **im** is used when it is followed by one of these letters: b, m, or p. An example is the word import.

(There are a few exceptions to these patterns. For example, we speak of a brass tray that is inlaid with silver. In the word inlaid, the variant form **il** is not found, even though the following part of the word, laid, begins with the letter l. Similarly, we speak of an inborn characteristic, meaning a characteristic that is born in a person, a natural characteristic. The variant form **im** does not begin the word inborn, even though the following part of the word, born, begins with the letter b. The exceptions are few.)

EXERCISE B in, im, il, ir?

1. **a.** inluminate **b.** illuminate ______
2. **a.** implicit **b.** inplicit ______
3. **a.** import **b.** inport ______

4. **a.** immerse **b.** inmerse ________________

5. **a.** inmolate **b.** immolate ________________

6. **a.** imbibe **b.** inbibe ________________

7. **a.** impeach **b.** inpeach ________________

8. **a.** illume **b.** inlume ________________

9. **a.** inplant **b.** implant ________________

10. **a.** inruption **b.** irruption ________________

The letters in, il, im, or ir at the beginning of a word do not always form the prefix **in** or one of its variant forms, **il**, **im**, or **ir**.

As in the case of other prefixes, we must look at the word part following these letters. Can it stand alone as a word? If not, can we substitute another prefix in place of the letters in, il, im, or ir and still have a word? If the answer to either of these questions is yes, then we are probably dealing with the prefix **in** or one of its variant forms, **il**, **im**, or **ir**.

EXERCISE C Prefix or Not?

1. inchworm ____________
2. ingress ____________
3. ingrow ____________
4. ink ____________
5. imp ____________
6. inform ____________
7. impound ____________
8. ire ____________
9. inhabit ____________
10. ill ____________

The prefix **in**, meaning in or into, as in the word income, may be confused with the prefix **in**, meaning not, as in the word indefinite, which means not definite. The prefix **in**, meaning not, has the same variant forms: **il**, **im**, and **ir.**

For the beginning students of English, the two prefixes, **in** and **im**, may cause trouble. However, more advanced students can usually decide which prefix they are dealing with. They may do this because they have developed a large vocabulary, or because they are skilled at guessing meaning from context–that is, they can understand the meaning of a word from the other words and sentences around it. They will try to see if the meaning in or into fits the word, or if the idea of not makes more sense.

Read this sentence: He was arrested for his illegal acts. The advanced student knows that the word legal means lawful. Which makes better sense in the sentence you have just read: He was arrested for actions that were not legal or not lawful or He was arrested for actions that were within or in the law? It is clear that the variant form **il** in this word is the prefix meaning not.

EXERCISE D in (in, into) or in (not)?

1. The children played indoors because of the bad weather outside. ____________
2. I can't tell you about the party because it was in-describable! ____________
3. A person who is inactive gains weight easily. ____________

4. His work is inaccurate because he is tired. ____________

5. This increase means she is the best-paid worker in the factory. ____________

6. He is indebted to me, but I am afraid he can never repay me. ____________

7. We will inoculate all children in the city with a vaccine to protect them from cholera. ____________

8. His teacher suggested that since his composition was very short, he could insert another paragraph between the second and third paragraph. ____________

A VOCABULARY WORKBOOK THRU READING

REVIEW OF SECTIONS 5, 6, 7, and 8

EXERCISE A Recall of Useful Words

com [Section 5.1]

1.____________ A relationship between two things [---rel---on]

2.____________ A group meeting regularly for some purpose [---mit---]

3.____________ A formal, organized meeting of a very large group [---ven---n]

4.____________ To gather together, usually with no formal organization [---g--gate]

5.____________ To exist at the same time or place [--e----]

6.____________ To crash together [---li-e]

de [Section 6.1]

1.____________ To state that someone or something is bad [--no--ce]

2.____________ A mood of unhappiness [--pr--sion]

3.____________ To give oneself to something [--vo-e]

4.____________ A reduction [--cl--e]

5.____________ To receive from a certain origin [--ri-e]

6.____________ A conclusion reached through the use of logic [--du---on]

ex [Section 7.1]

1.____________ To take out [--tr--t]

2.____________ To give out [-mi-]

3.____________ The act of carrying out a task or plan [--ecu-ion]

4.____________ Outside, outer [--t--nal]

5.____________ To shut out [--cl-de]

6.____________ To show [--po-e]

in [Section 8.1]

1.____________ To bring water in pipes to the land [--rig-t-]

2.____________ Money earned [--co-e]

3.____________ To express something indirectly [--p-y]

4.____________ To include, to make a part of [--vo-ve]

5.____________ To persuade [--d-c-]

6.____________ To make something clear by using an example [--lust-a-e]

EXERCISE B Recall of Useful Words

1. Marie Curie ________voted her life to science.
2. Her ________come has increased during the past ten years.
3. Farmers do not need to ________rigate their land where rainfall is heavy.
4. The president appointed a ________mittee to write a report on the situation.
5. There is no ________relation between a person's height and his or her salary.
6. Factories ________mit smoke that pollutes the air we breathe.
7. Should workers be ________volved in decisions made by managers and directors?

8. Very few words in English are ________rived from Chinese.
9. The news reporter ________posed the real cause of the accident.
10. On hot days, people ________gregate at the beach.
11. Feelings of ________pression may have physical causes.
12. A child running down the hall ________lided with old Mr. Jones.
13. We could not ________duce him to play cards with us.
14. The car's ________ternal appearance is bad, but the motor is in excellent condition.
15. Her smile ________plied that she thought we were not serious.
16. At the National ________vention of Dentists, Dr. Smith met his old friends from dental school.
17. He ________lustrated his strength by bending an iron rod with his bare hands.
18. Can a cat and a dog ________exist in a small apartment?
19. In the U.S.A., there has been a ________cline in the percentage of young people who smoke.
20. Enough silver can be ________tracted from this mine to make a fortune for the owners.

21. His own parents ________nounced him as a thief.

22. We went keep an open mind and not ________clude any possibility, if we want to solve the mystery of this death.

23. Her ________duction that her little boy had broken the plate turned out to be correct.

24. During his illness, the ________ecution of his business affairs became his son's responsibility.

EXERCISE C Using Prefix Meaning to Understand New Words

1. A strange concatenation of events led to his becoming president.

   a. happening inside the mind, an inner picture

   b. happening faster and faster

   c. the outer appearance only

   d. following each other, together like the links in a chain

2. In the accident, he was decapitated.

   a. A deep cut was made in his head.

   b. The upper part of his body was hurt badly.

   c. His head was cut off.

   d. He was thrown out of the car.

3. He didn't have time to reach the whole book; he just read an excerpt.
   a. the introduction
   b. a review or description of it
   c. a part taken from it
   d. a summary of it

4. She has an innate ability to speak different languages.
   a. great
   b. famous for it
   c. surprising
   d. born with it

5. Every time he exhaled, his chest hurt.
   a. breathed out
   b. lay down
   c. breathed in
   d. stoop up

6. The thief's confederate was a very clever person.
   a. a person who worked against him as an enemy
   b. a person that the thief stole money from
   c. a person who was older and more experienced
   d. a person who worked with him as a thief

7. During the war, they used chemicals to defoliate the trees.
   a. make the leaves grow thicker (so that they could hide from the enemy)
   b. make more branches grow out of the trees
   c. make the leaves fall off (so the enemy couldn't hide in the trees)
   d. make the trees grow taller at a faster rate

8. At the theater, John was so noisy that he was ejected by the manager.
   a. noticed, seen or heard clearly
   b. thrown out, driven out
   c. struck or hit with force
   d. put down, made to feel stupid

9. He was driving a decrepit car.
   a. noticeable, outstanding
   b. nice-looking on the outside
   c. broken down with wear and age
   d. larger and better than other cars

10. Mr. Jones was infuriated by the way his son spoke to him.

    a. put in a state of anger, enraged

    b. disappointed, his spirits lowered

    c. cheered up, his hopes raised

    d. left cold, without any feeling

9 pro

9.1 Meaning: before (in fronf of)

for (in favor of)

forward

EXERCISE A Deflnilions of Uscful pro Words

proceed	If we proceed in this way, we will soon reach our goal.
proclaim	In the old days, news was proclaimed by a town crier as he walked through the streets.
proposition	They were not interested in her proposition to buy their farm.
proslavery	It is difficult to think of a good proslavery argument.

promote Susan was promoted to the position of assistant manager because of her experience and her excellent relations with coworkers.

prospect He feels happy because of the prospect of a trip to France next year.

1.____________ In favor of slavery

2.____________ A thing that is expected to take place in the future (that which we look forward to)

3.____________ To declare in public, to announce publicly (to call forth)

4.____________ To go on, to advance (to go forward)

5.____________ To move someone to a higher position, rank, or class (to move someone forward)

6.____________ A plan, an idea, an offer, etc., presented for consideration (something put forward before others)

The letters *pro* at the beginning of a word will almost always be the prefix **pro**. An exception is a group of words that are formed with the prefix **proto**, meaning *earliest,* *first, original,* or *primitive.* You will not find many **proto** words in your dictionary, but you will see many **proto** words in your reading for university courses, because **proto** is a convenient combining form which writers of university textbooks need to make words that express certain ideas. For example, in a chapter on the history of astronomy, the writer may want to refer to the early stages of the science of astronomy. So she will coin, or make up, the word *proto-astronomy* to express this stage in its development. This word, *proto-astronomy,* is not in most dictionaries, but you are expected to figure out the meaning. Most such words are hyphenated.

Other, more commom **proto** words which are in the dictionary are usually *not* hyphenated. Examples are *prototype* and *protozoa.*

EXERCISE B Creating Words with proto

proto-agriculture

proto-subrine

proto-medicine

proto-Germanic

proto-tranquilizers

1.____________ Substances produced from plants by primitive people which, when eaten or drunk, produced a calm and happy mood

2.____________ The earliest attempts to produce food by raising crops rather than collecting wild plants that were found in the natural environment

3.____________ An early underwater boat from which our modern submarines were developed

4.____________ Related to the people who were the ancestors of the Germanic tribes

5.____________ Primitive methods of medical treatment used by early people

10 mis

10.1 Meaning: wrong, wrongly

EXERCISE A Definitions of Useful mis Words

misquote The senator was angry when a reporter misquoted the answer he had given to a question.

misbehavior She warned her children before their visit to her uncle that any misbehavior would be punished.

mistreat The British are famous for their quick anger if they see an animal mistreated.

misgovernment After ten years of misgovernment, the country needed economic help and firm leadership.

misfit John was a misfit on his uncle's farm last summer; he was too old to play with his cousins and too young to be friends with the children on the nearby farms.

misinterpret He misinterpreted her silence as a sign of dislike.

1.______________ A person who does not fit in; one who is poorly adjusted to his environ ment or to the people around him

2.______________ Actions that are not proper; the wrong way of acting

3.______________ Bad rule; wrong or poor government

4.______________ To draw the wrong conclusion, to understand or explain in the wrong sense

5.______________ To repeat someone's statement wrongly, to make a mistake in repeating what someone has said

6.______________ To abuse, to treat badly or wrongly

10.2 Spelling Problems and the Prefix mis

The prefix **mis** may cause spelling problems when the following word part begins with the letter*s*. Remember that the *s* of the prefix **mis** is never dropped. Therefore, the prefix **mis** and a word part beginning with the letter *s* means there will be a double *s*, as in the word *misspell.*

EXERCISE B Spelling Problems with mis Words

1. misspell ____________
2. misunderstand ____________
3. misspend ____________
4. misshapen ____________
5. misstep ____________
6. misdate ____________
7. misspelling ____________

10.3 Prefix or Not?

The letters *mis* at the beginning of a word do not always form the prefix **mis**. As you have learned in the preceding sections of this book, there are two tests for the prefix **mis**. Can the part that follows stand alone as a word? Or, can you substitute another prefix for **mis** and still have a word? If the answer to either of these questions is yes, then you are probably dealing with the prefix **mis**.

EXERCISE C Prefix or Not?

1.	**a.** misspell	**b.** mission	**c.** misspend	**d.** misstate
2.	**a.** misty	**b.** mistake	**c.** mistune	**d.** misteach
3.	**a.** misjudge	**b.** misdo	**c.** miser	**d.** mislike
4.	**a.** misshape	**b.** misfire	**c.** miscount	**d.** mishmash
5.	**a.** mistreat	**b.** mistrial	**c.** mistrust	**d.** mistletoe

The word part **miso**, meaning *hate,* may cause confusion for the student. For example, the word *misogamy* means hatred of marriage (and not wrong marriage), *misogyny* means hatred of women and *misanthropy* means hatred of all people[men and women].

The last example given, *misanthropy,* meaning hatred of people, is a word frequently used in books written for university-educated people. Also common are the other forms of this word: *misanthrope,* a person who hates people, and *misanthropic* (or *misanthropical*), the adjective forms of the noun. In this word you see a variant form of **miso**: **mis**, used because the following word part, *anthropy,* begins with a vowel.

You can avoid confusion between the prefix **mis**, meaning *wrong,* and the word part **miso**, meaning hatred, by simply memorizing the three examples given above: *misogamy, misogyny,* and *misanthropy.* These three words (and related forms such as *misanthrope, misogynist,* etc.) are the only commonly used words in English which contain the word part **miso**, meaning hatred.

It may happen that you will never see a **miso** word other than the three just mentioned. However, it may happen that you will read material written by someone who has used **miso** to express an idea that is very important in what he or she has written. Let us imagine that the author is writing about revolutionary movements or popular opposition to dictators and tyrants. Not wanting to keep repeating the phrase, hatred of tyranny, the writer will write *misotyranny.*

11 sub

11.1 Meaning: under, below, beneath

EXERCISE A Definitions of Useful sub Words

submerge In the fog, the little rowboat collided with a large passenger ship and instantly submerged.

subordinate She was sure that some male workers in the company were unhappy at being subordinate to a woman, but she handled this problem with great skill.

successor The successors to the old king was a young army officer who gave himself the title of Supreme Leader.

sufficient Are the resources of our planet sufficient for the needs of the coming century?

suppress In many cultures, men must suppress tears of pain or sorrow, which are considered a sign of femininity.

sustain In all the difficulties he faced, he was sustained by a deep trust in God.

1.____________ To keep from showing or expressing something (to keep under)

2.____________ To sink or go beneath the surface of the water, to disappear from sight by going under

3.____________ A person who follows another; someone who takes the job or position which another person has left

4.____________ To support, to help someone endure or bear something, to keep someone's spirit up (in other words, to hold someone up from below)

5.____________ Adequate, enough

6.____________ In a lower position, class, or rank

11.2 Variant Forms of the Prefix sub

suc, suf, sug, sup, sur

The prefix **sub** has several variant forms, depending on the beginning letter of the following word part.

suc If the prefix **sub** is used with a word part that begins with the letter *c,* the variant form **suc** is generally used, as in the word *successor.*

suf If the prefix **sub** is used with a word part that begins with the letter *f,* the variant form **suf** is generally used, as in the word *sufficient.*

sug If the prefix **sub** is used with a word part that begins with the letter *g,* the variant form **sug** is generally used, as in the word *suggest.*

sup If the prefix **sub** is used with a word part that begins with the letter *p,* the variant form **sup** is generally used, as in the word *suppress.*

sur If the prefix **sub** is used with a word part that begins with the letter *r,* the variant form **sur** is generally used, as in the word *surrender.*

EXERCISE B **Which Variant Form of the Prefix sub?**

1. mon ____________
2. press ____________
3. divide ____________
4. fuse ____________
5. round ____________
6. let ____________
7. ceed ____________
8. gest ____________
9. join ____________
10. side ____________

11.3 Variant Forms of the Prefix sub

sus The variant form **sus** is sometimes used when the following word part begins with one of these letters: *c, p,* or *t.* Here are some examples: *susceptible, suspend,* and *sustain.*

Sometimes the meaning of **sub** is more important in determining what form of this prefix to use than is the beginning letter of the following word part. It will help you to know that when the prefix **sub** is used to mean *beneath in rank,* its variant forms are not used. An example is the word *subconstable.* In addition, when **sub** is used to mean *a lower division,* its variant forms are not used. An example is the word *subgroup.*

EXERCISE C Which Form of sub?

1. **a.** submon **b.** summon ____________
2. **a.** submetallic **b.** summetallic ____________
3. **a.** subport **b.** support ____________
4. **a.** subprincipal **b.** supprincipal ____________
5. **a.** subspect **b.** suspect ____________
6. **a.** subregion **b.** surregion ____________
7. **a.** subceed **b.** succeed ____________
8. **a.** subconstable **b.** succonstable ____________
9. **a.** subfer **b.** suffer ____________
10. **a.** submerge **b.** summerge ____________
11. **a.** subgest **b.** suggest ____________
12. **a.** subpose **b.** suppose ____________
13. **a.** submitted **b.** summitted ____________
14. **a.** subchairman **b.** succhairman ____________

12 in

12.1 Meaning: not

EXERCISE A Definitions of Useful in Words

illegal	Driving a car through a red light is illegal.
improper	It was once considered improper for men to play tennis in shorts.
immature	Although her young brother is physically and socially immature, mentally he's an adult.
incapable	If they are incapable of reading on the advanced level, they should be given easier material.
infinite	Have you ever gone out to the country on a summer night and looked up at the infinite number of stars?
irrational	He has an irrational fear of cats.

1.____________ Against the law, not lawful

2.____________ Not able

3.____________ Not reasonable, not based on reason or logic

4.____________ Not suitable, not in good taste

5.____________ Without end, without limits, not measurable, not countable

6.____________ Not fully developed, not fully grown

12.2 Variant Forms of the Prefix in

il, im, ir

As in the case of other prefixes with variant forms, the prefix **in** may appear as **il**, **im**, or **ir** because of the beginning letter of the word part that follows it.

il The variant form **il** is used when the following word part begins with the letter *l*. An example is the word *illegal.*

ir The variant form **ir** is used when the following word part begins with the letter *r*. An example is the word *irrational.*

im The variant form **im** is used when it is followed by one of these letters: *b, m,* or *p.* Examples are *immature, impossible,* and *imbalance.*

EXERCISE B in, il, or ir?

1. **in** + balance ____________
2. **in** + animate ____________
3. **in** + convenient ____________
4. **in** + effective ____________
5. **in** + patient ____________
6. **in** + measurable ____________
7. **in** + regular ____________
8. **in** + sane ____________
9. **in** + replaceable ____________
10. **in** + secure ____________

The letters *in, il, im,* or *ir* at the beginning of a word do not always form the prefix **in** or one of its variant forms, **il, im,** or **ir.**

As in the case of other prefixes, we must look at the word part following these letters. Can this word part stand alone as a word? If not, can we substitute another prefix in place of the letters *in, il, im,* or *ir* and still have a word? If the answer to either of these questions is yes, then we are probably dealing with the prefix **in** or one of its variant forms, **il**, **im**, or **ir**.

A VOCABULARY WORKBOOK THRU READING

REVIEW OF SECTIONS 9, 10, 11, and 12

EXERCISE A Recall of Useful Words

pro [Section 9.1]

1.____________ In favor of slavery [---sl-----]

2.____________ A thing looked forward [---sp--t]

3.____________ To announce publicly [---cl--m]

4.____________ To go on [---c--d]

5.____________ To move someone to a higher position [---m-t-]

6.____________ A suggestion, etc., presented before others [---po--tion]

mis [Section 10.1]

1.____________ A person who does not fit in with the people around him or with his environment [---f--]

2.____________ An improper way of acting [---be---ior]

3.____________ Bad rule [---gov-------]

4.____________ To understand in the wrong sense [---in---pret]

5.____________ To repeat someone's statement incorrectly [---qu--e]

6.____________ To abuse [---tr--t]

sub [Section 11.1]

1.____________ To keep from expressing [---pr--s]

2.____________ To sink under [---m--ge]

3.____________ One who follows another in a certain position [---ce--or]

4.____________ To help someone bear something or endure [---t--n]

5.____________ Adequate, enough [---fi----t]

6.____________ In a lower position [---or--nate]

in [Section 12.1]

1.____________ Not lawful [--le--l]

2.____________ Not able [--ca--ble]

3.____________ Not based on reason or logic [--ra---nal]

4.____________ not in good taste [--pro--r]

5.____________ Without an end or limit [--fi--te]

6.____________ Not fully developed [--ma--re]

EXERCISE B Recall of Useful Words

1. Psychologists say that ________behavior may be a child's way of getting the attention of his or her parents.
2. A person who constantly ________presses anger, rather than expressing it in a harmless way, may become physically ill.
3. A dog can communicate with its owner, but it is ________capable of saying that last night's dimmer was better than tonight's.
4. The grains of sand on a beach are ________finite.
5. A common ________slavery argument is that if slaves are well treated, they do not want their freedom.
6. If you ________interpret the first sentence in a paragraph, you may have trouble understanding the rest of it.
7. They drove north for two miles and then ________ceeded west.
8. There is ________ficient food on this table for at least four people.
9. When victory over their enemy was ________claimed, people danced in the streets.
10. It is ________legal to drive on the left side of the road in America, but not in English.

11. Many sea animals live on rocks that are ________merged at high tide but exposed at low tide.
12. Adults sometimes behave ________maturely.
13. Some people study because of the ________spect of an examination; others, because of genuine interest.
14. Who will be the ________cessor to the present chairman of the board when he retires next year?
15. When Mary was ________moted, she moved to a larger office with a rug on the floor.
16. We all have ________rational fears, but we manage to live normal lives in spite of them.
17. Every citizen must be alert for signs of __________ government.
18. When he was angry, he ________treated his dog.
19. They disagreed as to their ________ordinate goals, but there was no argument over their major goal.
20. Because the vice-president was ________quoted, people thought she was in favor of a plan which she actually opposed.
21. Her ________position was accepted by all the members of the committee.
22. Because there were no ________fits in the class, the students worked well together and enjoyed each other's company.

23. He told a joke which his aunt thought was ________ proper.

24. Whenever he became discouraged, he was ________ tained by his wife's confidence in him.

EXERCISE C Using Prefix Meaning to Understand New Words

1. Your argument is *irrefutable.*

   a. is in favor of your own ideas

   b. is under discussion

   c. is better than any other argument

   d. cannot be answered

2. I don't like the *subservient* way he acts.

   a. like the leader of our group

   b. like a servant or someone in a low position

   c. without taste or good manners

   d. coldly, as if he is apart from us

3. The actors moved to the *proscenium.*

   a. the back or inner part of the stage

   b. the area in the theater just below the stage, where an orchestra is sometimes found

c. the part of the stage that sticks out in front of the curtains

d. the middle area of the stage

4. John was playing cards with his friends. He said, *Misdeal!*

   a. These cards have been dealt wrongly.

   b. the cards you dealt me are excellent.

   c. The cards you dealt me are all of the same kind.

   d. The cards you dealt me are not interesting.

5. Mary has a *propensity* for algebra.

   a. liking

   b. hatred

   c. lack of interest

   d. no ability or talent

6. The students were surprised by the *misprint.*

   a. a word printed in very small letters

   b. a word printed in very large letters

   c. a word printed wrongly

   d. a missing word that was not printed

7. Some day everybody will learn about his *illicit* actions.

a. without sense, stupid

b. low, mean, base

c. not lawful, against the law

d. generous, done for others

8. The *substructure* of a building is important.

a. area in front

b. outer walls

c. design or plan

d. foundation, lower part

9. I think you are acting under a *misapprehension.*

a. control of someone else

b. wrong understanding

c. favorable idea or opinion

d. first or most important plan

10. Susan had trouble reading the *prolegomena.*

a. final section

b. notes printed at the bottom of the page

c. words carved in stone

d. introductory section

13 re

13.1 Meaning: back; again

EXERCISE A Definitions of Useful Words

revival In many Western countries, there is a revival of interest in making pottery, knitting sweaters, and weaving cloth–all by hand.

restrict Because of his poor health, his activities were restricted.

restoration Mary is the director of a special team of experts working on the restoration of several buildings which were constructed in the seventeenth century.

reject John rejected his parents' offer to buy him a car, as he wanted to be completely independent.

recurrent War seems to be a recurrent problem of civilization, although we all wish for its final disappearance.

reveal When the company Susan worked for went through a period of reorganization, she was revealed as a capable and loyal department head.

1.____________ To turn down; not to accept (to throw back)

2.____________ The act of bringing to life again, of paying attention to something that was forgotten or neglected

3.____________ The act of bringing something back to its original condition; making something look the way it was when it was new

4.____________ To show something that was previously hidden (to take the veil back)

5.____________ Appearing again; coming back from time to time

6.____________ To limit; to keep within certain limits (to keep back)

13.2 Prefix or Not?

The letters *re* at the beginning of a word do not always form the prefix **re**. As in the case of other prefixes, we must look at the word part following these two letters. Can it stand alone as a word? Can a different prefix be substituted, producing a word? If the answer to either of these questions is yes, then we are probably dealing with the prefix **re**.

14 un

14.1 Meaning: not; the reversal of an action

EXERCISE A Definitions of Useful un Words

unattainable A person should have goals which he or she can achieve, but perhaps everyone also needs to have an unattainable goal.

unceasing Although she was neither educated nor very intelligent, her unceasing efforts to do her best led to success.

unorthodox Almost every great idea in science and religion was rejected as unorthodox by the society in which it first appeared.

unconfirmed There was an unconfirmed report in the university newspaper that the dean of students had accepted a new position at a college in France.

untie	In the story she was reading, the hero was captured and bound with ropes by his enemies, but he managed to untie his bonds during the night and escape.
unjustifiable	Many people believe that striking a child is unjustifiable, no matter what the situation.

1.____________	Inexcusable; such that no reason can be given to show that it is right or good; characteristic of an action which cannot be shown to be fair or right
2.____________	Not capable of being reached or achieved
3.____________	To loosen bonds, to set free (to reverse the action of tying)
4.____________	Never stopping; continuous
5.____________	Not standard, not approved, nor conventional or traditional
6.____________	Not supported as the truth by official sources; not declared true by the authorities or people concerned

The letters *un* at the beginning of a word usually form the prefix **un**, meaning *not*.

There are two exceptions. One is the large group of words that begin with the prefix **under**(*underneath, underline,* etc.). These words are easy to recognize. The other exception is the group of words that begin with the prefix **uni**, meaning *one.* If the letters *un* are followed by the letter *i,* the prefix may be either **un**(*not*) or **uni**(*one*). Fortunately, **uni** words are few in number, and a student of English on the advanced level knows most of them.

15 trans

15.1 Meaning: across; beyond

EXERCISE A Definitions of Useful trans Words

transcontinental	The construction of a transcontinental railroad across the United States meant a reliable and fast way to travel or ship goods from the east to the west coast.
transplant	Doctors have succeeded in transplanting almost every organ of the human body, including the heart.
transliterate	It is difficult to transliterate Arabic names, because some sounds in Arabic do not exist in English and so cannot be easily represented by the letters used to write English.
transparent	His face was like a transparent piece of glass, revealing his inner emotions.

transcend	Can people transcend their selfish nature and love others as they love themselves?
transfer	Mary was happy when the computer firm she worked for in New York decided to transfer her to their office in Mexico City.

1.____________	Across a continent; extending across the surface of a continent from coast to coast
2.____________	To go beyond the limits; to rise beyond one's power
3.____________	To represent or spell words in a different alphabet
4.____________	To remove a living organism or part of an organism from one place and put it in another, to grow or function there
5.____________	To remove, send, or carry from one place to another
6.____________	Clear; allowing light rays to pass through so that things can be clearly seen through it

When the prefix **trans** is followed by a word that is capitalized, it is usually separated from this word by a hyphen, as in the word *trans-Siberian.* Two common exceptions to this rule are the words *transatlantic* and *transpacific.*

16 ob

16.1 Meaning: against, facing

EXERCISE A Definitions of Useful ob Words

opponent Without a good opponent, a tennis player does not play his best game.

objective Susan's objective was a new car, and by taking a second job, she was able to earn and save the necessary money within a year.

obstacle There is no easy road to success, no path without obstacles.

offend Robert was offended when he was not invited to the party.

obvious The solution to the problem was obvious —even a child could see it.

obligation Parents have an obligation to raise their children so that as adults, they can succeed in their work and in their relationships with others.

1.____________ Clear, easily seen (facing one)

2.____________ One who is on the other side in a contest; a person who is against one

3.____________ A thing standing in one's way; a hindrance (against one)

4.____________ A duty

5.____________ To cause someone to feel hurt; to annoy; to wound (to push or hit against)

6.____________ An aim; a goal or target to be aimed at (a target to throw against)

16.2 Variant Forms of the Prefix ob

oc, of, op, o

The prefix **ob** has several variant forms, depending on the beginning letter of the word part that follow it.

oc If this letter is *c,* the variant form **oc** is used, as in the word *occur.*

of	If the letter is *f,* the variant form **of** is used, as in the word *offend.*
op	If the letter is *p,* the variant form **op** is used, as in the word *opponent.*
o	If the letter is *m,* then the letter *b* of the prefix **ob** is dropped, and the variant form **o** is used, as in the word *omit.*

There are exceptions to these patterns, but they are few.

EXERCISE B ob, oc, of, op, or o?

1. **ob** + mission ____________
2. **ob** + fend ____________
3. **ob** + durate ____________
4. **ob** + struct ____________
5. **ob** + fer ____________
6. **ob** + pose ____________
7. **ob** + stacle ____________
8. **ob** + posite ____________
9. **ob** + clude ____________
10. **ob** + tain ____________

A VOCABULARY WORKBOOK THRU READING

REVIEW OF SECTIONS 13, 14, 15, and 16

EXERCISE A Recall of Useful Words

re [Section 13.1]

1.____________ To refuse to accept [--j--t]

2.____________ The act of bringing to life again [--v---al]

3.____________ Bringing something back to its original condition [--st--ation]

4.____________ To show something that has been hiden [--v--l]

5.____________ Returning from time to time [--cu--ent]

6.____________ To keep something within limits [--str--t]

un [Section 14.1]

1.____________ Inexcusable [--j----fiable]

2.____________ Not capable of being achieved [--att---able]

3.____________ To set free [--t-e]

4.____________ Never stopping [--ce--ing]

5.____________ Not standard, not traditional [--or---dox]

6.____________ Not declared true by the authorities [--conf--med]

tran [Section 15.1]

1.____________ Across a continent [-----con------al]

2.____________ To go beyond one's limits or power [-----ce-d]

3.____________ To spell words in a different alphabet [-----lit--ate]

4.____________ To move part of an organism from one place and put it in another [-----pl--t]

5.____________ To move or send from one place to another [-----f--]

6.____________ Clear, so that objects can be seen through it [-----par---]

ob [Section 16.1]

1.____________ Clear, easily seen [--v---s]

2.____________ A person who is against one [--pon--t]

3.____________ A thing in one's way [--sta---]

4.____________ A duty [--lig-----]

5.____________ To annoy or hurt [--f--d]

6.____________ An aim or goal [--j---ive]

EXERCISE B Recall of Useful Words

1. His ________ceasing cheerfulness, strangely enough, began to annoy us.
2. In ________ferring the goods from the boat to the truck, the workers stole about 10 percent of the shipment.
3. The ________ponents sat silently, staring at the pieces on the chess board.
4. His application for a visa was ________jected by the consul.
5. There was an ________confirmed story going around among the workers that the owner intended to sell the factory.
6. Susan had three ________stacles to overcome in her struggle to get a law degree: she was a foreigner, she was a woman, and she was over forty.
7. I'm sorry if I have ________fended you, he said.
8. In America today, there is a ________vival of interest in picnics and other activities that involve the extended

family–that is, parents, grandparents, aunts, and uncles.

9. It was hard for him to ________literate his name the first time he did it: Negmeddin Seifullah Shaheen. The letters made his name seem strange.
10. She ________stricted herself to attending only one movie a week because of her studies.
11. Can a woman's heart be ________planted into a man's body?
12. Because it was hot, he ________tied his tie and took off his jacket.
13. They promised not to ________veal his secret.
14. Although it is ________vious that there is a connection between cigarette smoking and lung cancer, people continue to smoke.
15. The doctor noticed ________current cases of influenza, particularly among his older patients.
16. Your ________jective is to expand your vocabulary.
17. The ________storation of the old palace was difficult, as it had been neglected for a long period and then used as a cigarette factory for ten years.
18. The packaging, ________parent plastic bags, allowed shoppers to examine the fruit.

19. Her ________orthodox ideas may not always work, but sooner or later her originality will be recognized and appreciated.
20. Medical treatment was ________attainable in his village, so he was taken to a nearby city.
21. Shakespeare's heroes and heroines have ________cended time, for they remain forever alive in his great plays.
22. In America, ________continental television may mean the end of regional or local entertainment.
23. She thought it was ________justifiable for him to express his anger by kicking the dog.
24. The members of any society have ________ligations to each other.

EXERCISE C Using Prefix Meaning to Understand New Words

1. The land which the government had seized ten years earlier *reverted* to the original owners.

   a. was given back

   b. was sold

   c. was asked for

   d. was not returned

2. That's an *unconventional* idea.

   a. excellent, superior

   b. wrongly expressed

   c. not ordinary, not common

   d. against logic

3. It was a *transpolar* flight.

   a. around the equator

   b. in the outer layer of the atmosphere

   c. under the moon, by moonlight

   d. across the north or south pole

4. They *uncovered* the dish.

   a. did not cover

   b. covered it again

   c. wrongly covered it

   d. took the cover off

5. He *retracted* his promise to take the children to the zoo.

   a. wrongly promised

   b. took back his promise

   c. was the first to promise

   d. did not promise

6. They listened to his *objection.*

   a. argument against something

   b. argument in favor of something

   c. a wrong or poor argument

   d. an argument that is excellent

7. This window is *translucent.*

   a. It prevents light from coming through.

   b. It is in favor of light–that is, it makes the light stronger.

   c. Light comes through it.

   d. Light is reflected or turned back from it.

8. I don't like to listen to an *obloquy.*

   a. a speech in favor of or praising someone

   b. a speech without a purpose

   c. a speech for a wrong or poor purpose

   d. a speech against or attacking someone

9. They *replenished* their food shelves.

   a. filled them up again

   b. moved them across the room

   c. put them down in a lower position

   d. took the food away

10. She is hard to argue with because she is *obstinate.*

    a. lacking intelligence

    b. standing firm against all arguments

    c. wrong in her thinking

    d. beyond others in intelligence

17 ab

17.1 Meaning: from; away

EXERCISE A Definitions of Useful ab Words

abduction	The abduction of a child is one of the most horrible crimes a person can commit.
abnormally	Everyone behaves abnormally to some degree at some point in life, but to what degree, and how often?
abrupt	His abrupt departure did not give them a chance to thank him for the gifts he had brought them.
abstain	A feature of most religions is a regularly recurring period during which the faithful abstain from eating certain foods, or fast completely.
absorb	Young minds absorb knowledge as a sponge absorbs water.

abstract	We can understand and accept death as an abstract destiny for all, but few people can face with calm the prospect of their own immediate death.

1.____________ Unexpected, sudden

2.____________ General, as opposed to particular; theoretical, as opposed to real and particular (drawn away from what is real)

3.____________ The act of kidnapping or taking a person away by force

4.____________ Not normally; strangely; irregularly (away from what is normal)

5.____________ To soak up, to take in, to suck up

6.____________ To keep from participation; to refrain or hold back voluntarily (to hold from or to hold away)

17.2 Variant Forms of the Prefix ab

abs, a

The prefix **ab** occurs in variant forms, depending on the beginning letter of the word part following it.

abs If this letter is c or t, then the variant form **abs** is used, as in the words abscond and abstain.

a If the beginning letter is v, then the b of **ab** is dropped, and the variant form **a** is used, as in the word avocation.

EXERCISE B ab, abs, or a?

1. **ab** + duct ______________
2. **ab** + tain ______________
3. **ab** + tract ______________
4. **ab** + breviate ______________
5. **ab** + solve ______________
6. **ab** + vert ______________
7. **ab** + sorb ______________
8. **ab** + cond ______________
9. **ab** + negate ______________
10. **ab** + tention ______________
11. **ab** + errant ______________
12. **ab** + cess ______________

17.3 Prefix or Not?

The letters ab at the beginning of a word do not always form the prefix **ab**. Can the word part that follows stand alone as a word? Can a different prefix be substituted, producing a word? If the answer to either one of these questions is yes, then the prefix **ab** is probably present.

18 inter

18.1 Meaning: between, among

EXERCISE A Definitions of Useful inter Words

interval Mary taught school from 1974 to 1976, and then from 1978 to the present date. In the interval, she got her master's degree in biology.

intermediate Many Third World countries have a technology which is not advanced but which cannot be described as primitive, so it is spoken of as intermediate.

intercept Susan, the best player on the basketball team, is skillful at intercepting the ball when players on the opposing team try to pass it to each other.

interject Holding up his hand to silence his friends, he said, Please! May I just inter-

	ject this one remark?
intermittently	Rain fell intermittently during the night.
intercede	When the director of John's department dismissed him because of his poor work, John asked the assistant director to intercede for him.

1.____________ Starting and stopping; periodic; stopping for a time periodically

2.____________ A space of time between two conditions or events

3.____________ To stop a speaker by saying something; to break into someone's speech, or one's own speech

4.____________ Being in the middle; lying between two limits or extremes

5.____________ To take or seize something while it is on its way between the sender and the receiver

6.____________ To go or act between two people, usually on behalf of one of them, to settle a difference or quarrel

The prefix **inter** does not present any special problem to native or non-native speakers of English. However, a student examining **inter** words should take note of the prefix **intra**, meaning within or inside. What is the difference between an intercollegiate tennis tournament and an intracollegiate tennis tournament? Which tournament involves the players of only one college? The answer to the last question is: an intracollegiate tennis tournament.

EXERCISE B inter or intra?

1. What word would you use to describe a problem between several states in the United States?

   a. interstate **b.** intrastate ________________

2. What word would a biologist use in describing the different parts of one cell?

   a. intercellular **b.** intracellular ________________

3. What word would be used to describe a movie star who is known all over the world?

   a. international **b.** intranational ________________

4. Which word is used by a doctor in speaking of injections into a muscle rather than into a vein?

   a. intermuscular **b.** intramuscular ________________

5. Which word is used by a doctor in speaking of injections to be made into a vein?

   a. intervenous **b.** intravenous ________________

6. Which word would be used by an anthropologist in writing about a problem concerning several tribes?

   a. intertribal **b.** intratribal ________________

7. Which word would be used by state lawmakers in discussing a proposed law to regulate traffic in their state?

   a. interstate **b.** intrastate ________________

8. Which word would be used by a zoologist in discussing the spread of a certain type of fish from one ocean to another?

   a. interoceanic **b.** intraoceanic ________________

9. Which word would be used by a chemist in discussing a reaction between different parts of the same molecule?

   a. intermolecular **b.** intramolecular ______________

10. Which word would be used to describe the movement of people from one continent to another?

    a. intercontinental **b.** intracontinental ___________

18.2 inter (between, among) or in (in, into)?

The prefix **inter**, meaning between or among, and the prefix **in**, meaning in or into, are seldom confused, because the letters inter at the beginning of a word almost always form the prefix **inter**. One important exception is the word internal, meaning inner or in. In this word, the prefix is not **inter**, but **in**.

19 mono and poly

19.1 mono, meaning one or alone

EXERCISE A Definitions of Useful mono Words

monotony	Because human beings dislike monotony, the same delicious dinner, if repeated every day, will become distasteful.
monopoly	Manufacturers who enjoy a monopoly can charge as much as they like for their product.
monologue	John never really talks with other people; when he meets someone, he begins a monologue, which is interrupted only when the other person leaves.
monogamy	Monogamy is the usual marital pattern in most Western societies.
monosyllable	Some people express their anger by silence, or by speaking only in monosyllables.

monotheistic	Three great monotheistic religions were born in the Middle East: Judaism, Christianity, and Islam.

1.____________ A word of one syllable

2.____________ A long speech or talk made by one person

3.____________ Sameness, or lack of variety

4.____________ Related to or characterized by the belief that there is only one God

5.____________ Marriage with only one person at a time

6.____________ Exclusive or sole control of the supply or production of any kind of goods or services

19.2 poly, meaning many

EXERCISE B Definitions of Useful poly Words

polygamy	Polygamy is a feature of marriage in many societies.
polytheistic	In some polytheistic religions, the gods are represented in the form of animals.

polyglot In a city like Vienna, it is easy to find polyglots.

polysyllabic When John wrote his first composition in his freshman English class, he used many polysyllabic words, in an effort to display his vocabulary

polygon Modern architects have abandoned the square and the rectangle, preferring to create buildings that are based on circles, triangles, and polygons.

polyclinic Nadia is a young doctor working at a polyclinic, where she gets a broad medical experience.

1.____________ A hospital or clinic for many kinds of diseases

2.____________ Related to religions based on a belief in several or many gods

3.____________ A person who speaks several languages

4.____________ Related to words made up of several syllables

5.____________ Marriage with more than one wife at a time (or more than one husband, although this is rare and usually known as polyandry)

6.____________ A figure having many sides and angles (usually more than four angles)

20 anti

20.1 Meaning: against, opposing

EXERCISE A Definitions of Useful anti Words

antisocial Adolescents may go through an antisocial period, when they read a great deal or listen to tapes and records alone in their room.

antidote The container of any poisonous substance that is used in the home should bear a statement as to the nature of the poison, and the antidote that should be taken if it is swallowed by mistake.

antislavery It is difficult in the spirit of antislavery that exists today to understand how Plato could have accepted slavery as natural, even necessary.

antagonist In most novels, the hero's antagonist is hateful in some way, so that the reader enjoys that person's eventual defeat.

antipathy It is unfortunate that a person may arouse our antipathy by resembling someone we dislike.

antithesis A woman's personality may be the antithesis of her husband's, yet their marriage may be a happy one.

1.____________ Not caring for the company of others, not sociable (against society)

2.____________ Feelings of dislike or hostility (feelings against someone)

3.____________ Being against slavery

4.____________ A substance or medicine taken as a remedy against a poison; a substance taken to counteract the effects of poison

5.____________ The exact opposite

6.____________ A person who opposes or struggles with another

20.2 Using a Hyphen with the Prefix anti

The prefix **anti** is separated from the following word part by a hyphen when the word part begins with the letter i, as in the word anti-intellectual, or when it is capitalized, as in anti-Christian.

20.3 The Prefix anti and the Prefix ante

The prefix **anti**, meaning against, should not be confused with the prefix **ante**, meaning before.

The difference in spelling will inform us whether we are dealing with an **anti** word or an **ante** word. One exception is the word anticipate (with its derivatives anticipatory, anticipation, etc). Knowing that this word means to expect something and also to introduce ahead of time, you can guess that it is an **ante** word with an exceptional spelling.

The difference in spelling usually prevents confusion between the prefix and **anti** and **ante**. However, both prefixes are pronounced the same, so in listening, we must decide whether the speaker has used a word beginning with the prefix **anti** or **ante**.

EXERCISE B anti or ante?

1. Because ________war protests and demonstrations received such widespread support, the government was forced to reconsider its participation in the Vietnam conflict.

2. In the centuries ________cedent to the Industrial Revolution, changes in society and culture took place only very slowly.

3. The labor movement in the early 1900s made very few gains; in fact, ________labor laws allowed factory owners to continue to exploit workers cruelly.

4. The ________war period was a time of frantic preparation for battle with a powerful enemy.

5. Scientists all over the world waited with fearful ________cipation for the practical application of the discovery of nuclear fission.

REVIEW OF SECTIONS 17, 18, 19, and 20

EXERCISE A Recall of Useful Words

ab [Section 17.1]

1.____________ Sudden, unexpected [--r--t]

2.____________ General rather than particular [--str--t]

3.____________ The act of kidnapping [--duc----]

4.____________ Not normally [--n-----ly]

5.____________ To soak up [--s--b]

6.____________ To refrain from participation [--st--n]

inter [Section 18.1]

1.____________ Starting and stopping, not continuous [-----mi--ently]

2.____________ A period between two events or conditions [-----v--]

3.____________ To break into someone's speech [-----j--t]

4.____________ Between two extremes [-----med--te]

5.____________ To seize something while it is on its way, before it reaches its destination [-----ce-t]

6.____________ To go between two people on behalf of one of them [-----ce-e]

mono [Section 19.1, Exercise A]

1.____________ A word of one syllable [----s-------]

2.____________ A talk or speech made by one person [----lo-ue]

3.____________ Sameness, lack of change [----to-y]

4.____________ Characterized by the belief that there is only one God [----th----ic]

5.____________ Marriage with only one person at a time [----ga--]

6.____________ Exclusive control of the supply or production of any kind of goods or services [----p--y]

poly [Section 19.2, Exercise B]

1.____________ A hospital for many kinds of diseases [----cl---c]

2.____________ Related to religions based on a belief in several or many gods [----th----ic]

3.____________ A person who speaks several languages [----g--t]

4.____________ Related to words made up of several syllables [----s-----ic]

5.____________ Marriage with more than one wife at a time [----g--y]

6.____________ A figure having many sides and angles [----g--]

anti [Section 20.1]

1.____________ Not caring to be with others [----so---l]

2.____________ A feeling of dislike [----pa--y]

3.____________ Being against slavery [----s------]

4.____________ A substance taken to act against the effects of poison [----d-t-]

5.____________ The opposite [----th--is]

6.____________ A person who struggles against another [---ago-ist]

EXERCISE B Recall of Useful Words

1. To escape ________tony, people sometimes accept changes that are actually harmful.
2. An ________social mood may strike even the friendliest, most outgoing person.
3. All week, ________mittent gunfire was exchanged by the two opposing groups, but there was no direct, decisive battle.
4. The dry soil ________sorbed the brief rainfall, but more was needed to save the crops.
5. Many people ________stain from alcoholic drinks because of their religious beliefs.
6. Her daughter is a ________glot who speaks fluent English, Germany, and French.
7. During the ________val between the first and second acts, he drank a glass of lemonade.
8. He's in an English class at the ________mediate level.
9. In a second language, we may seem ________rupt, because we do not know the little phrases that introduce a change in topic.
10. Certain animals are ________gamous, such as the greylag goose, which is faithful to its mate for life.

11. In most cities, the government has a ________poly on utilities such as gas and electric power.
12. Often it is the mother who ________cedes with the angry father on her son's behalf after the two have had a conflict.
13. We need an ________dote for the strain of city life, which has a poisonous effect on our mind and body.
14. The line between normal and ________normal behavior is hard to draw.
15. Sometimes students consider their teacher an ________gonist.
16. The police ________cepted the thieves before they reached the border.
17. His behavior is the ________thesis of kindness or concern for others.
18. Is ________duction for political purposes ever justifiable?
19. Reading the newspaper aloud, he ________jected a short, witty comment that made his listeners laugh.
20. For a short while after her divorce, she felt an ________pathy for every man she met.
21. The little girl constructed a giant ________gon with her building blocks.

22. Money in the ________stract interests an economist; the rest of us think in terms of whether our salary will allow us to buy a car or take a trip.
23. People in the ________slavery movement in America were called abolitionists, since they were fighting for the abolition of (doing away with, ending) slavery.
24. The speaker's use of ________syllabic words made her audience think she was well educated.
25. ________theism preceded ________theism in the history of religion.
26. A ________logue is boring unless the speaker is charming, or funny, or both.
27. At a ________clinic, doctors see a wide variety of medical problems.
28. We speak in ________syllables when we talk to very young children.

EXERCISE C Using Prefix Meaning to Understand Words

1. It is strange to think that an antibiotic drug can help a sick person.

   a. made of many different substances

b. injuring or destroying life

c. supporting or favoring good health

d. made of a single substance

2. A car owner doesn't want to clean the car with an abrasive material.

   a. wearing away or rubbing off the paint

   b. not effective, not useful

   c. highest in price

   d. below the usual standard

3. The sound of the sad monody made the listeners feel sad, too.

   a. song played by several musical instruments

   b. song that comes before the action on the stage

   c. song without feeling or emotion

   d. song sung by one person

4. This animal is polydactylic.

   a. has a large cranium (skull)

   b. has no vertebral column (spine, backbone)

   c. has only one ocular organ (eye)

   d. has many digits (fingers, toes)

5. The king died when his son was only two years old. The boy became king when he was twenty. In the interregnum, his uncle ruled.
   a. the land inside the walls of the palace
   b. the land beyond or outside the palace walls
   c. period between the king's death and his son's becoming king
   d. any country that is wrongly or poorly governed

6. The money in that country is monometallic.
   a. all the coins are made of one kind of metal
   b. the coins are made of a mixture of several metals
   c. the coins are below their usual value
   d. the coins are made of a substance, such as plastic, that is not metal

7. In the garden, red flowers were interspersed with yellow ones.
   a. planted very early, before summer
   b. set here and there among the others
   c. surrounded on the outer edge
   d. taken away and replaced by others

8. He stole the company's money and absconded.

   a. never worked again

   b. was killed [cut down]

   c. went away secretly

   d. behaved wrongly

9. His aberrant behavior attracted attention.

   a. holding closely to what pleases oneself

   b. going against what others want or desire

   c. continuing in one fashion or way, regardless of circumstances

   d. wandering away from what is normal or correct

10. It was a polychromatic painting.

    a. of very high quality

    b. poorly done

    c. in several colors

    d. out of or away from modern style

21 syn

21.1 Meaning: with; together

EXERCISE A Definitions of Useful syn Words

symmetry The outer appearance of the human body is an example of natural symmetry, because the right half is like the left.

symptom A symptom common to almost every disorder or disease of the human body is a feeling of being tired, a lack of energy.

synthetic The use of synthetic fibers to make cloth means that land can be used to grow food crops instead of cotton.

symbol All over the world, the dove is the symbol of peace.

sympathy It is not necessary to use words to express sympathy for someone in trouble–a warm look of understanding or a smile means much more.

synonym Because of the varied linguistic forces which have shaped English, we have many pairs of synonyms, such as *adore* (of Latin origin) and *worship* (of Anglo-Saxon origin).

1.____________ Artificial; made by people (made by putting things, such as chemicals, together)

2.____________ A word having almost the same meaning as another

3.____________ A change in the body indicating a disease or disturbance in function.

4.____________ The act of sharing the feelings of another, especially the resultant emotion this may cause; pity or compassion

5.____________ A sign of something else, especially a visible sign of something invisible, such as an idea or a quality

6.____________ Correspondence or matching in size, shape, and position of two parts that are on opposite sides of a real or imaginary driving line

21.2 Variant Forms of the Prefix syn

The prefix **syn(syl, sys, sym)** appears in variant forms according to the beginning letter of the word part that follows it.

syl If this letter is *l,* the variant form **syl** appcars, as in the word *syllable.*

sys If the letter is *s,* the variant form **sys** appears, as in the word *system.*

sym The variant form **sym** appears if the following word part begins with one of these letters: *b, m,* or *p.* Examples are the words *symbol, symmetry,* and *sympathy.*

EXERCISE B syn, syl, sym, or sys?

1. phony ____________
2. thetic ____________
3. agogue ____________
4. chronize ____________
5. biosis ____________

6. logism ____________
7. sarcosis ____________
8. metallism ____________
9. opsis ____________
10. tax ____________

22 dis

22.1 Meaning: apart from; separation; not

EXERCISE A Definitions of Useful dis Words

diverse	The woman of today has diverse recreational interests, which may range from chess to deep-sea diving.
diffusion	The diffusion of a new idea through modern means of mass communication, such as television, is both quick and far-reaching.
dispute	If a dispute results in some solution acceptable to both parties, relations between them may be better than they were before, since the air has been cleared.
dissolve	In some parts of the world, a marriage can be dissolved almost as easily as a spoonful of sugar in a glass of water.

distinct On moonless nights, the outline of building against the sky is not distinct.

distribution It has been said that everybody is dissatisfied with his or her share of the world's wealth, but that nobody complains about the distribution of intelligence.

1.____________ Clear, clearly seen (separated from other things, marked out)

2.____________ Varied, of various kinds; different (separate)

3.____________ The act of spreading, scattering

4.____________ The act of giving out portions; allotment (giving out separate shares)

5.____________ A quarrel

6.____________ To bring to an end; to cause to pass into solution so that the original form is lost (to set loose into separate parts)

22.2 Variant Forms of the Prefix dis

dif The prefix **dis(dif, di)** appears in variant forms according to the beginning letter of the following word part. If this letter is *f,* the variant form **dif** is used, as in the word *diffusion.*

di The other variant form, **di**, generally appears when the following word part begins with one of these letters: *g, l, m, r,* or *v.* Examples are the words *diverse* and *dilate.* However, there are many exceptions to these patterns, such as the words *dislocate* and *dismember.*

EXERCISE B dis, dif, or di?

1. **dis** + late __________
2. **dis** + like __________
3. **dis** + fraction __________
4. **dis** + comfort __________
5. **dis** + tract __________
6. **dis** + gest __________
7. **dis** + lute __________
8. **dis** + fer __________
9. **dis** + gust __________
10. **dis** + cover __________

22.3 The prefix dis and the Prefix di

The variant form **di** of the prefix **dis** is sometimes confused with the prefix **di**, meaning *two,* as in the word *dictionary,* meaning *a division into two parts.*

If you are trying to guess the meaning of an unfamiliar word beginning with the letters *di* perhaps the idea of *two* should be tested. If it seems to fit the sentence, the prefix must be **di**, meaning *two.* If the idea of *two* doesn't seem reasonable for this particular sentence, try the meaning *not* or *away.* Perhaps it is a **dis** word.

23 non

23.1 Meaning: not

EXERCISE A Definitions of Useful non Words

nonintervention The leaders of small countries ask the great powers to keep their promise of nonintervention in their internal affairs.

nonsense A person who writes nonsense in his or her native language will probably write nonsense in any second language that person learns.

nonconformist Young people are nonconformists when judged by the standards of the older generation, but they do conform to patterns of behavior common to their own generation.

nondescript A criminal is often a nondescript person whom witnesses can never recall clearly.

noncommittal It is difficult to give a noncommittal answer in a second language–even saying nothing is more difficult in a second language than in one's mother tongue.

nonproductive Is daydreaming nonproductive? Or is it a mental activity that is necessary for our emotional health?

1.____________ Not entering an argument or quarrel in order to settle it; not interfering

2.____________ Not useful; without worthwhile results

3.____________ A person whose behavior is not like that of others

4.____________ Something which is silly or without meaning

5.____________ Not showing agreement or disagreement; refusing to indicate approval or disapproval

6.____________ Not easily described; having no outstanding characteristics or features

23.2 Using a Hyphen with the Prefix non

When the prefix **non** is used before a word that is capitalized, a hyphen separates it from the word. An example of such a hyphenated word is *non-Italian.*

EXERCISE B **Hyphenated or Not?**

1. epidemic ____________
2. English ____________
3. Arab ____________
4. federal ____________
5. European ____________
6. Indo-European ____________
7. oriental ____________
8. Japanese ____________
9. Christian ____________
10. Moslem ____________

23.3 The Prefix non (not) and the Prefix non (nine)

The letters *non* at the beginning of a word almost always form the prefix **non**, meaning *not.* Although the prefix **non**, meaning *nine,* is identical in spelling, it is not a source of confusion, because it occurs in only a few words, and because the meaning of *nine* is usually made clear by the context–that is, the sentence in which it occurs and the sentences before and after it.

Notice the italicized word in this sentence: Susan knew several elderly people, including one *nonagenarian.* This is one of the few words that begin with the prefix **non**, meaning *nine.* The word *nonagenarian* refers to someone who is ninety years old, or between ninety and one hundred years old.

24 mal

24.1 Meaning: bad, wrong

EXERCISE A Definitions of Useful mal Words

maladjusted Some psychologists believe that the treatment of a maladjusted child cannot be successful unless all members of the child's family are treated.

malicious To explain natural disasters such as floods and earthquakes, primitive people told stories about malicious supernatural creatures who wanted to hurt humans.

malady Imaginary maladies may bring wanted attention and care to the sufferer.

malefactor Malefactors may be sent to prison, but upon their release, they may return to their former activities.

malnutrition	It is not only the poor who suffer from malnutrition–it is anyone who is ill-informed about what a healthy diet is.
malediction	In many Mediterranean countries, it is believed that a malediction pronounced by certain people can cause bad fortune, illness, or even death.

1.____________	Faulty diet (bad or wrong diet)
2.____________	With evil intentions or motives; done with ill will (in a bad spirit)
3.____________	Any disease of the human body (bad condition)
4.____________	Out of harmony with others (badly adjusted)
5.____________	A curse; the opposite of a blessing (bad words)
6.____________	A wrongdoer; a criminal

24.2 Prefix or Not?

The letters *mal* at the beginning of a word do not always form the prefix **mal**. Can the following word part stand alone as a word? Can another prefix be substituted, producing a word? If the answer to either of these questions is yes, the letters *mal* are probably the prefix **mal**.

REVIEW OF SECTIONS 21, 22, 23, and 24

EXERCISE A Recall of Useful Words

syn [Section 21.1]

1.____________ Not occurring in nature, made by people [---th--ic]

2.____________ A word meaning almost the same as another [---on--]

3.____________ A change in the body showing a disease or illness [---pto-]

4.____________ Pity or warm feeling for another [---pa--y]

5.____________ A visible sign of something invisible, such as an idea or quality [---bo-]

6.____________ Correspondence in size and position of two parts that are on opposite sides of an imaginary dividing line [---m-tr-]

dis [Section 22.1]

1.____________ Clearly seen [---t--ct]

2.____________ Varied [--ve-se]

3.____________ The act of spreading [---f-sion]

4.____________ The act of giving out shares or portions [---tr--ut---]

5.____________ A quarrel [---p-t-]

6.____________ To bring to an end; to pass into solution so that the original form is lost [---s--ve]

non [Section 23.1]

1.____________ Not interfering [---in---vention]

2.____________ Not producing results [---pr-----ive]

3.____________ A person whose behavior is not like that of others [---conf--mist]

4.____________ Something without meaning or sense [---s----]

5.____________ Not showing agreement or disagreement [---c--mit--l]

6.____________ Not easily described because of lack of outstanding features [---de----pt]

mal [Section 24.1]

1.____________ Poor diet [---n--------]

2.____________ Done with evil intentions [---ici--s]

3.____________ Any disease [---a-y]

4.____________ Poorly adjusted [---adj-----]

5.____________ A curse [---ed--tion]

6.____________ A wrongdoer [---efac--r]

EXERCISE B Recall of Useful Words

1. Women do not want to wear ________thetic jewels, no matter how beautiful they are.
2. Severe ________nutrition can damage a child's brain.
3. Mary gave ________committal answers when asked about her plans, because she wanted to keep them secret for a while.
4. The ________fusion of the printing process, making books available to all, was a tremendous step forward in the spread of knowledge.
5. The collection and ________tribution of workbooks seems more like a privilege than a duty to children in school.

6. She is suffering from a strange ________ady that cause her to grow shorter in the summer months.
7. Is the sixth sentence in this exercise ________sense?
8. The cross is a ________bol of Christianity.
9. The ________icious gossip of the old men who met at the club every morning made them feared and hated.
10. A ________onym for the word *brave* is the word *courageous.*
11. Salt ________solves faster in hot water than in cold.
12. Her husband was a ________descript little man, but she was a tall, unforgettably beautiful woman.
13. With his angry father's ________ediction ringing in his ears, he ran out of the apartment and down the stairs.
14. The letters were not ________tinct because the paper had gotten wet.
15. A common ________ptom of low blood pressure is dizziness.
16. Jealousy is a ________productive emotion.
17. In the West, people express their ________pathy by sending flowers to parents who have lost a child.
18. Not all ________efactors go to prison; unfortunately, the police do not catch every criminal.

19. A policy of ________intervention in the affairs of neighboring countries was declared by the new president.
20. Words in English are derived from ________verse language.
21. A ________adjusted child often becomes an unhappy adult.
22. During the ________pute, John lost his temper and pounded the table with his fist.
23. He is a ________conformist in dress, but his ideas are surprisingly orthodox.
24. Her cleaning woman insisted on ________metry, always putting the ashtray in the exact center of the desk, with the books in two neat stacks, one on each side.

EXERCISE C Using Prefix Meaning to Understand Words

1. With friendly smiles, the little group *disbanded.*
   - **a.** met together
   - **b.** went forward
   - **c.** broke up, separated
   - **d.** went back

2. One of the oldest *synagogues* in the world is in Cairo.
   a. walls that separate the city from the area around it
   b. roads that cross each other
   c. places on the river where boats stop to load or unload
   d. places where Jews meet together for religious worship

3. He talked *nonstop* for two hours.
   a. in a very low voice
   b. not pausing
   c. with great feeling
   d. in an evil or bad manner

4. When the child put the toy into a box and shook it, it *disintegrated.*
   a. fell to the floor
   b. fell apart, broke into pieces
   c. fell out of the box
   d. fell together with the box

5. He looked at me *malevolently.*
   a. evilly, with bad will
   b. without any feeling
   c. through a window
   d. not recognizing me

6. Schools should be *nonpartisan.*

   a. advanced, forward

   b. against what is bad

   c. not controlled by political parties

   d. under governmental control

7. As the years passed, the principles of the two branches of the church were *syncretized.*

   a. separated, kept apart

   b. wrongly understood

   c. given first place

   d. fused, put together

8. As the ship sailed into rough water, Mary experienced a certain *malaise.*

   a. feeling bad or ill

   b. feeling of excitement

   c. lack of feeling

   d. feeling of separateness of body and mind

9. They *divested* him of his uniform.

   a. gave him the wrong uniform

   b. made his uniform like the standard uniform

c. spoke against his uniform

d. took off his uniform

10. She gave birth to a *malformed* baby.

a. incompletely developed

b. below the usual standard

c. abnormal, badly formed

d. better or beyond the usual standard

Chapter II ▸▸ Roots and Suffixes

25 dic, dict
26 ton, tain, tin
27 cep, cap, ceive, cept, capt, cip
28 fac, fic, fit, fact, fect, fict
29 log, logy
30 gress, grad
31 gen, gener
32 ject, jact
33 mit, miss
34 ced, cess, ceed
35 plic, plex, pli, ply
36 pon, pos, pound
37 spect, spec, spic
38 graph, gram
39 mot, mob, mo
40 cred, credit
41 duc, duct
42 stat, sta, stit, sist
43 tend, tens, tent
44 fer, lat

25 dic, dict

25.1 Meaning: say, speak; word

EXERCISE A Definitions of Useful dic Words

contradict Mr. Smith said that his children did not watch TV very much, but his wife contradicted him, declaring that they spent hours in front of the TV set.

dictator Ask anyone to name a dictator of our century, and the answer will probably be Hitler.

dedicate The new school building was dedicated to Lorene Hitt Lusher, a much-loved woman who had taught in the community for thirty years.

edict An edict of the health department concerning the cleanliness of restaurants was

	followed by surprise inspections made by health department officials.
diction	The careful diction of a foreign language teacher in the classroom may be very different from his or her normal speech among friends.
indicate	Careless work may indicate dislike of the job or of the employer.

1.____________	One who rules with absolute, supreme power or authority (one who speaks with authority or power)
2.____________	To state of declare the opposite
3.____________	To show or point to, to be a sign of (to tell)
4.____________	Manner of pronunciation or speech
5.____________	To declare something in honor of
6.____________	A public notice, rule, or order issued by authority (something declared, said)

26 ten, tain, tin

26.1 Meaning: hold, keep

EXERCISE A Definitions of Useful ten Words

maintenance In calculating the total cost of owning and using a car, you must think of the cost of the car itself, insurance, license, fuel, and maintenance.

retain Although she could not read or write, she could retain a long list of names and addresses in her mind.

attainment The most striking attainment of modern medicine is the heart transplant.

continent When the English refer to the continent, they usually mean Europe.

untenable He could not win the argument because his ideas were untenable.

detain	She was detained by an unexpected visitor, and as a result, she arrived late for the meeting.

1.____________ Not capable of being defended of held

2.____________ To keep back, to delay

3.____________ The act of keeping property or equipment in good condition for use

4.____________ One of the six large divisions of land in the world (land that is continuous or held together)

5.____________ Achievement, accomplishment

6.____________ To hold or keep

27 cep, cap, ceive cept, capt, cip

27.1 Meaning: to take

EXERCISE A Definitions of Useful cep Words

perceive	When they perceived that they had been tricked, they were angry.
capacity	What is the capacity of this container?
conception	Her conception of England will change if she ever travels there.
reciprocal	There is a reciprocal agreement between the two countries.
conceive	We cannot conceive of a world without love.
captive	During the war, some captives escaped from their prison camps.

1.______________ Mutual

2.______________ To understand, to notice

3.____________ One who is held as a prisoner especially in war.

4.____________ To imagine

5.____________ A mental picture or idea

6.____________ Amount of power to take and hold

28 fac, fic, fit fact, fect, fict

28.1 Meaning: to do or make, produce

EXERCISE A Definitions of Useful fac Words

factor	Labor and capital are two important factors in industry.
beneficial	Sunshine and fresh air are beneficial
unification	The unification of all countries in Europe is the dream of many young people.
efficient	She is an efficient worker, but she does not get along with others.
insignificant	What seems like an insignificant amount of money to one person may be a fortune to another.
infect	A small cut on his finger became infected, causing serious illness.

1.____________ One of the things that contribute to produce a result

2.____________ Not important (making no difference)

3.____________ Very capable; able to do something quickly and well

4.____________ Advantageous, giving helpful or good results (doing good)

5.____________ The act of making several units into one unit; the act of uniting

6.____________ To harm with disease-producing germs (bacteria, microbes)

A VOCABULARY WORKBOOK THRU READING

REVIEW OF SECTIONS 25, 26, 27, and 28

EXERCISE A Recall of Useful Words

dic, dict [Section 25]

1.__________ One who rules with absolute power [----at--]

2.__________ To state or declare the opposite [--ntra----]

3.__________ To be a sign of [i----ate]

4.__________ Way of speaking or pronouncing [----ion]

5.__________ To declare something in the honor of [de------]

6.__________ A public order, rule [e----]

ten, tain [Section 26]

1.__________ Not capable of being protected or held [u----ab--]

2.__________ To delay, keep back [d-----]

3.______________ Keeping property or equipment in good condition [main---an--]

4.______________ One of the six large divisions of land in the world [c-----ent]

5.______________ Achievement, accomplishment [at----m---]

6.______________ To hold or keep [r-----]

cep, cap, ceive, cept, capt, cip [Section 27]

1.______________ Mutual [r----roc--]

2.______________ To understand, to notice [p-----ve]

3.______________ One who is held prisoner [----ive]

4.______________ To imagine [c------e]

5.______________ A mental picture or idea [c------ion]

6.______________ Amount of power to take and hold [---acit-]

fac, fic, fit, fact, fict, fect [Section 28]

1.______________ One of the things that cause an effect [----or]

2.______________ Not important [--signi------]

3.______________ Capable, working well [ef---ie--]

4.______________ Giving good results [b--e---ia-]

5.____________ The act of making several units into one unit [--i---ation]

6.____________ To harm with microbes that cause disease [i-----]

EXERCISE B Recall of Useful Words

1. An important ________tor in many happy marriages is a similarity in background of husband and wife.
2. Europe is a con________ent.
3. He was put into prison because he disobeyed the king's e________.
4. John became very nervous whenever his wife contra____________ed him.
5. The bene________ial results of a long vacation include eagerness to return to work.
6. When he was halfway finished packing the suitcase for his trip, he realized that its ________acity was less than he had thought.
7. Is there such a thing as a good ________ator? The answer to this question is probably no.

8. The two families had a re________rocal baby-sitting arrangement.
9. Some people believe that dreams of falling in________ate lack of security or self-confidence.
10. Over a five-year period, the main ________ance of a large computer may cost as much as the original purchase price.
11. If humans are unhappy as ________ives, how do animals in the zoo feel?
12. At the concert, the singer de________ated her final song to her first music teacher.
13. Perhaps the uni________ation of all transport systems under one powerful authority would solve the city's traffic and transportation problem.
14. His ________ion was so careless that the children could not understand what he said.
15. He emigrated at the age of twenty, so he re________ed his command of his mother tongue, even though it was not spoken in his new country.
16. Centuries ago, our con________ion of the universe was very different from what it is today.
17. An ef________ient woman can combine marriage and a career, if her husband is cooperative.

18. In today's world, the argument that men are superior to women is un________able.
19. If you go out on a summer evening and look at the stars, you will realize how insigni________ant your problems are.
20. She per________ed that beneath a hard, unfriendly-seeming outer shell, her neighbor was a kind and gentle person.
21. George finally learned to control his temper, an at________ment that made him a much better husband and father.
22. Although the wound was deep, it was not in________ted, and the injured person recovered quickly.
23. It is easier to con________of a united Europe than a united world.
24. They would have talked longer with Dr. Jones, but they knew she was on her way to the airport and they didn't want to de________ her.

EXERCISE C Using the Meaning of Roots to Understand Words

1. He was *indicted* for murder.
   a. put in prison
   b. killed by a murderer
   c. accused by legal authorities
   d. taken by the police

2. As a computer operator, she was extremely *proficient.*
   a. well paid, receiving a high salary
   b. skillful, able to do something expertly
   c. sought after, wanted by several companies
   d. admired, looked up to by others

3. The average university teachers is interested in *tenure.*
   a. the right to hold a job permanently
   b. a salary that increases each year
   c. the right to take a year's leave of absence
   d. the freedom to change one's job

4. He was pleased by their *reception* of his idea.
   a. understanding, comprehension

b. carrying out, putting into effect

c. taking for consideration

d. supporting, upholding

5. An *artificial* Christmas tree stood near the door.

a. tall, stretching upward

b. evergreen, keeping its green color

c. large, taking up a lot of space

d. not natural, made by people

6. The baby *captivated* his grandmother.

a. won her by his charm

b. drove her away

c. had an effect on

d. looked at

7. She was interested in the *artifacts* of the ancient Greeks.

a. things they said

b. things they held to be true

c. things they made

d. things they took from others

8. Her handbag was *capacious.*

a. made partly or completely by hand

b. large enough to take many things

c. kept close or held tightly

d. described as or said to be good

9. The *tenants* of this house are wealthy.

a. people who construct or make buildings for others

b. people who are found nearby, neighbors

c. people who receive payment of rent for their property

d. people who occupy or hold a house in exchange for rent

10. He thought of his aunt as his *benefactress*

a. one who receives affection and trust

b. one who does good or helpful things for another

c. one who holds a higher position in age or rank than another

d. one who speaks well of others

29 log, logy

29.1 Meaning: word, speech, reason, study

EXERCISE A Definitions of Useful log words

analogy	Today some writers draw an analogy between the world and a spaceship, since both have limited room, resources, and energy, and therefore can take care of only a limited number of people.
logical	Every day we perform hundreds of actions that do not require logical thinking, because we do them by force of habit.
ideology	Americans like the Russian people, although they fear their communist ideology.
archaeologist	When the archaeologist Howard Carter first looked through a small hole into Tutankhamen's tomb, he said, I see wonderful things!

apologize People usually apologize if they arrive late for an appointment.

theology The history of the greatest universities of the West shows that in each case, the first faculty established was the faculty of theology.

1.____________ A specialist in the study of [ast human life and culture, as shown by the monuments, etc., of ancient peoples

2.____________ To express regret for some improper or harmful remark or act

3.____________ A relation of similarity between two things, not in appearance, but in circumstances or effects

4.____________ The study of religion

5.____________ Manner of thinking or set of ideas characteristic of an individual, a social class, or a nation

6.____________ In accordance with the reasoning power of the mind

30 gress, grad

30.1 Meaning: to step or go

EXERCISE A Definitions of Useful gress Words

congress	The Congress of the United States is composed of two parts: the Senate and the House of Representatives.
gradual	The change in her personality was so gradual that it was not noticed by her family at first.
digress	The speaker digressed for a moment to tell a story about his childhood.
transgression	He asked God to forgive him for his transgression.
regression	When a child is tired or ill, there may be a regression in behavior–that is, the child may act like a boy.

degradation The story was about an alcoholic who refused to admit that he had a drinking problem until he reached the depths of degradation.

1.____________ A sin; a violation of a law or command (going beyond)

2.____________ The body of representatives of a nation which makes the laws of the nation (people who go or act together)

3.____________ Act or process of the lowering of physical, moral, mental, or social levels (going down)

4.____________ A return to an earlier level or stage (going back)

5.____________ Proceeding or changing in slow stages (steps) that are not clearly marked

6.____________ To turn aside from the main subject in speaking or writing (to step aside)

31 gen, gener

31.1 Meaning: birth, race, kind

EXERCISE A Definitions of Useful gen Words

genetics Before the development of genetics, it was believed that blood was the carrier of heredity.

genesis The genesis of the development of steam power took place when a certain young boy watched a pan of water boiling on the stove.

regeneration After a year of hard work, a person needs a vacation for the regeneration of the spirit and the ability to enjoy life.

gender In many languages, nouns have gender; that is, they are masculine or feminine.

congenital Today doctors can operate on the tiny heart of a newborn infant with a congenital heart disorder.

indigenous Potatoes and tomatoes are not indigenous to Europe but were brought there shortly after the first contacts with North and South America.

1.____________ Existing at, or dating from, birth

2.____________ Produced, growing, or living naturally in a certain country or climate; native (born in it)

3.____________ The coming into existence (birth) of anything

4.____________ Sexual classification: male or female (kind)

5.____________ The branch of biology which deals with heredity, so-called because the genes are the carriers of heredity

6.____________ Re-creation, rebirth, or revival; restoration to the original strength or condition

32 ject, jact

32.1 Meaning: to throw

EXERCISE A Definitions of Useful ject Words

objective	If the judge's son is on trial in his father's courtroom, the judge cannot be objective.
eject	Because of his shouting, he was forcibly ejected from the room.
conjecture	Scientists make conjectures and then test them to see if they are correct.
object	Anyone who objects to the plan is free to draw up a new one.
projectile	Today there are weapons which can send a projectile accurately towards a target which is 3,000 miles away.

1.____________ Not prejudiced, without any tendency to view things emotionally or unfairly

2.____________ A guess; a theory based on a guess

3.____________ To throw forward in time or space

4.____________ Something thrown forward by force; a missile

5.____________ Expel, throw out, drive out

6.____________ To oppose, to disapprove, to declare opposition (to throw against)

A VOCABULARY WORKBOOK THRU READING

REVIEW OF SECTIONS 29, 30, 31, and 32

EXERCISE A Recall of Useful Words

log, logy [Section 29]

1.____________ A specialist in the study of the life and culture of ancient peoples [--chaeo---ist]

2.____________ To express regret for a harmful or improper act [apo------]

3.____________ A relation of similarity in the circumstances or effects of two things [-na----]

4.____________ The study of religion [--eo----]

5.____________ Manner of thinking or set of ideas characteristic of an individual, a class, or a nation [-deo----]

6.____________ In accordance with the reasoning power of the mind [---ic-l]

gress, grad [Section 30]

1.____________ A sin; lawbreaking, crime [tr--------ion]

2.____________ The lawmaking body of representatives of a nation [c-------]

3.____________ The lowering of one's physical, moral, mental, or social level [de--------n]

4.____________ A return to an earlier level or stage [-------ion]

5.____________ Changing in slow stages that are not clearly marked [------l]

6.____________ To turn aside from the main subject in speaking or writing [-i-----]

gen, gener [Section 31]

1.____________ Existing at, or dating from, birth [con-----al]

2.____________ Produced, growing, or living naturally in a certain country or climate [in-----ous]

3.____________ The coming into existence of anything [----si-]

4.____________ Sex classification: male or female [---d--]

5.____________ The branch of biology which deals with heredity [----t---]

6.____________ Rebirth or revival; restoration to the original condition or strength [re------tion]

ject, jact [Section 32]

1.____________ Not prejudiced, without a tendency to view things emotionally or unfairly [ob-------]

2.____________ A guess, or a theory based on a guess [con-------]

3.____________ To throw forward in time or space [-ro----]

4.____________ Something thrown forward by force; a missile [-ro-----le]

5.____________ Expel or throw out [-j---]

6.____________ To oppose or disapprove [-bj---]

EXERCISE B Recall of Useful Words

1. In his lecture on the history of Spain, the speaker di________ed to describe a summer vacation he had spent there.

2. While mango trees are indi________ous to India, they are now grown in many other countries.
3. The archaeo________ist is investigating a city that was once important but today is only broken bricks and dust.
4. This pro________ile is guided by a small electronic device, so that it can follow and hit a moving target.
5. In spite of their con________ures that she would fail, Mary succeeded.
6. When Susan accidently broke John's typewriter, he was so angry that he would not accept her apo________.
7. Is it wrong for scientists in the field of ________etics to try to develop a better human being?
8. The president of the little republic could not succeed in getting the national con________ to accept his ideas and make them laws.
9. The doctor studied the history of her patient's illness and on that basis pro________ed its probable development over the next few years.
10. Biologists and doctors often make an ana________between the human heart and a pump.
11. If we cut off a dog's tail, no re________ation will take place.

12. Is it true that a materialistic ideo________ controls our actions today?
13. There was a ________ual improvement in her work.
14. He had lied and stolen, and now that he was planning to kill, he realized that his moral de________ation was complete.
15. A child suffering from con________ital deafness has great difficulty learning to talk.
16. Many people ob________ to scenes of violence in television programs.
17. Is it true that women, because of their experience in solving the problems of managing a home and caring for children, are more ________ical than men?
18. Not all trans________ions of the law are equally serious.
19. It is very difficult to determine the ________der of a newly hatched chick[baby chicken]
20. Serious conflict between husband and wife may require the ob________ive viewpoint of a marriage counselor, so that a solution to the problem can be reached.
21. The pilot's seat can be e________from the newest fighter plane if the pilot sees that he cannot land safely.
22. What is the ________esis of language?

23. Will an atomic war mean a re________ion from civilization to the life of cave dwellers?

24. Should we expect experts in theo________ to be better than the rest of humanity?

EXERCISE C Using the Meanings of Roots to Understand Words

1. It is difficult to deny the correctness of this *syllogism.*
   a. an action or deed for the welfare of humanity
   b. a step forward taken with others in a series of steps
   c. an argument presented according to a certain system of reasoning
   d. a view or way of looking at something

2. This is the *centigrade* system of measuring temperature.
   a. reasonable, logical
   b. creating or giving rise to good results
   c. made or carried out by a machine
   d. on a scale consisting of a hundred steps or divisions

3. He is like his *progenitors.*
   a. observes, onlookers

b. words describing or telling about a person

c. deeds, things done by someone

d. ancestors, forefathers

4. *Miscegenation* is not against the law in the United States.

   a. moving up by steps from the bottom of the social scale to the top

   b. speaking or writing on a scientific subject without a college degree

   c. throwing new or valuable objects out of the house

   d. intermarriage or interbreeding of people of different races

5. This is a *retrograde* development.

   a. going from better to worse

   b. seen or noticed easily

   c. praised or spoken of highly

   d. causing or creating other developments

6. The audience was very interested in Charles Brown's *monologue.*

   a. a long speech by one person

   b. an act without words, the actor using only his body

c. a series of dance steps done very slowly

d. an act in which small objects are thrown into the air

7. On this small island, every home has its own *generator.*

a. a pump that sprays or throws out a substance that kills mosquitos

b. a machine that creates or produces electricity

c. a boat that moves easily in water that is not deep

d. a system of pipes to carry drinking water

8. At the farewell party, Mary *injected* a bit of humor.

a. appreciated, enjoyed

b. saw, observed

c. introduced, threw in

d. accepted, took in

9. To show films, we need a *projector.*

a. a room or hall to hold the audience

b. a machine to throw the picture onto a screen

c. a source of light

d. a film made of a series of steps of action pictures

10. This novel is famous for its *prologue.*

a. action, movement of the story

b. originally, creativity, fresh view

c. the preface or introduction

d. the length or number of pages it contains

33 mit, miss

33.1 Meaning: to send, let go

EXERCISE A Definitions of Useful mit Words

commit	People may be so committed to their work that they neglect family responsibility.
transmit	News is instantly transmitted to all parts of the world, thanks to highly developed means of communication.
permissive	In the treatment of their children, parents fall into one of two categories: permissive or strict.
submit	Some older employees are unwilling to submit to the orders of a young supervisor.
missile	Cave dwellers threw rocks at each other, but the missiles of today are the products of scientific and industrial technology.

missive An important missive from one government to another may be carried by the ambassador personally.

1.____________ To yield or surrender

2.____________ A letter (something sent)

3.____________ To bind or tie

4.____________ To send or transfer from one place or person to another

5.____________ An object thrown (sent) with intent to hurt or destroy

6.____________ Lenient; the opposite of strict or harsh

34 ced, cess, ceed

34.1 Meaning: to go, move along

EXERCISE A Definitions of Useful ced Words

procedure	In unusual or extreme cases, the normal procedure is not followed by the surgeon performing an operation.
precedent	In arguing a client's case in court, a lawyer will refer to a similar case where a judge's decision established a precedent in his client's favor.
proceedings	The proceedings of club meetings are recorded by a secretary.
secede	A civil war may take place if part of a nation attempts to secede and set up an independent government.
procession	A funeral procession moves along slowly.

antecedent In the years antecedent to World War II, Germany built up its military forces.

1.____________ Going or occurring before; at an earlier time

2.____________ Something done or said that serves as a rule or example for similar cases in the future (something that occurred or went before)

3.____________ A particular manner or method of carrying out an operation or course of action (the way to move forward)

4.____________ A group of people moving onward in an orderly manner; a parade

5.____________ To withdraw from an organization or federation, especially from a political body (to move aside)

6.____________ The minutes or records of meetings of a society, club, board, etc. (what went on)

35 plic, plex, pli, ply

35.1 Meaning: to fold, lay together

EXERCISE A Definitions of Useful plic Words

duplicate	A photocopy machine can duplicate a letter of several pages in less than a minute.
implicit	His satisfaction with the restaurant was implicit in the large tip he gave the waiter.
complex	There are no simple answers to complex problems.
pliant	A sapling, or baby tree, is of course more pliant than one that is fully mature.
accomplice	The police could not understand how he had robbed the bank without an accomplice.
replica	Sometimes a replica is so well made that only an expert can distinguish it from the original.

1.____________ A partner or helper in a criminal act (someone drawn in or folded in)

2.____________ To make a copy of something

3.____________ Understood or expressed indirectly, not spoken (not open, but folded in)

4.____________ The opposite of simple (with folds)

5.____________ Easily bent, flexible (able to be folded)

6.____________ A reproduction or copy, as of a picture or statue

36 pon, pos, pound

36.1 Meaning: to put or place

EXERCISE A Definitions of Useful pon Words

compound Hydrogen sulphide is a compound of sulphur and hydrogen.

postulate Young people often ask this question: If we postulate an all-powerful but merciful God, then how can we explain the existence of evil?

component One of the components of a successful party is good food.

dispose of A city can dispose of its garbage[rubbish] in ways that are beneficial or in ways that are completely wasteful and possibly harmful.

exposition Many cities have a large open area where trade fairs, industrial expositions, etc., are held.

proponent	Few people are proponents of higher taxes.
1.____________	To start with a certain assumption that is claimed to be true and is accepted without proof (to put forward)
2.____________	An ingredient or part of something (what is put with something)
3.____________	A substance formed by the union or mixture of elements or parts (things put together)
4.____________	An advocate or supporter (one who puts something or someone forward)
5.____________	To get rid of (to put away or put aside)
6.____________	A public show or exhibit (things put out to be looked at)

A VOCABULARY WORKBOOK THRU READING

REVIEW OF SECTIONS 33, 34, 35, and 36

EXERCISE A Recall of Useful Words

mit, miss [Section 33]

1.____________ To yield or surrender [su----]

2.____________ A letter [-----ve]

3.____________ To bind or tie [c-----]

4.____________ To send or transfer from one place or person to another [tr------]

5.____________ 1An object thrown to hurt or destroy [-----le]

6.____________ The opposite of strict [per-------]

ced, cess, ceed [Section 34]

1.____________ At an earlier time [ante-----t]

2.____________ An act or decision that serves as a rule or example [pre-----t]

3.____________ A method of doing something [p-----ure]

4.____________ A group of people moving as if in a parade [p------ion]

5.____________ To withdraw, as from a political body [se----]

6.____________ The minutes of a club, society, etc. [p------ings]

plic, plex, pli, ply [Section 35]

1.____________ A partner or associate in crime [acc------e]

2.____________ To make a copy [du-----te]

3.____________ Expressed without words or indirectly [im-----t]

4.____________ The opposite of simple [c-----x]

5.____________ Flexible, easily bent [---ant]

6.____________ A reproduction or copy of a picture, a statue, etc. [r-----a]

pon, pos, pound [Section 36]

1.____________ To start with an assumption that is claimed to be true [---tu----]

2.____________ An ingredient or part of something [c-----ent]

3.____________ A substance formed by the union of elements or mixture of parts [c------d]

4.____________ A supporter or advocate [p-----ent]

5.____________ To get rid of [dis---- of]

6.____________ A public exhibit or show [ex----tion]

EXERCISE B Recall of Useful Words

1. At their monthly meeting, the club members usually dis________ed of old business before they took up any new business.
2. The two men were accom________es in crime.
3. The teenage children of strict parents envy the children of per________ive parents.
4. In accident Greece, important news was trans________ted by swiftly running messengers.
5. What is the best pro________ure for changing a flat tire?
6. Did you see anything interesting at the ex________ition?
7. The chief com________ent of this mixture is milk.
8. The pro________ings of the meeting were kept secret.
9. Can a woman who is a mother be as com________ted to a career as a man who is a father?

10. By paying for the medical expenses of the man she struck with her car, Mrs. Jones im________itly admitted her responsibility for the accident.
11. There was a civil was when Biafra attempted to se________e from Nigeria.
12. Dr. Smith found it very difficult to deal with such a com________ subject in a short lecture.
13. Most arsenic com________s are dangerous.
14. All the younger brothers sub________ted to the oldest son.
15. The ________ive was sent by a special messenger.
16. At the head of the pro________ion were the oldest and most respected members of the community.
17. Anyone can see that this is a re________a instead of the real thing.
18. She is a pro________ent of free university education.
19. They ________tulated the necessity of cooperation in the development of an agricultural society.
20. There is no pro________ent at this university for the admission of a student who has not graduated from secondary school.
21. In their battle with the police, the students used bricks as ________iles.

22. The secretary used carbon paper to du________ate the letter.

23. Humans were hunters in the thousands of years ante________ent to the development of agriculture.

24. A snake moves gracefully because its body is _______ant.

EXERCISE C Using the Meanings of Roots to Understand Words

1. An economic *mission* from the U.S. made a study of the problem.
   a. persons holding responsible positions
   b. persons put under someone's control
   c. persons sent to do a special task
   d. persons folding or meeting together

2. He *conceded* the fact that they were wrong.
   a. held to, insisted on
   b. went along with, agreed to
   c. stood against, denied
   d. covered up, hid

3. The pianist *transposed* the song.
   a. repeated it
   b. put it in a different key (musical scale)
   c. went through it quickly
   d. memorized it

4. They watched the dark clouds *receding*.
   a. carrying rain
   b. growing larger
   c. moving away
   d. releasing rain

5. Some palm trees have *plicate* leaves.
   a. folded like a fan
   b. made of several parts that are put together
   c. having sharp points
   d. growing longer each year

6. A serious gardener keeps a *compost* heap or pile.
   a. a substance thrown out to kill insects
   b. a supply of seeds that produce fast-growing plants
   c. several books that explain the best gardening methods
   d. several things put together to enrich the soil

7. He is writing a book about his *ancestors.*
   a. the people who went before him, his forefathers
   b. the people who held out or fought against him
   c. the things he has done
   d. the ideas he wants to spread or send out into the world

8. The table was made of *plywood.*
   a. a substance that resembles wood but is actually plastic
   b. a substance made of plants that are put or mixed together like a paste that hardens to resemble wood
   c. wood that is treated in a series of steps so that it is extra strong
   d. wood made of very thin sheets of wood that are laid or stuck together

9. When the armies of the two countries approached each other, the United Nations *interposed* a special unit of U.N. soldiers.
   a. took away from between
   b. made larger, increased
   c. put in between
   d. watched or observed

10. He served as the king's *emissary.*

a. a person who holds power

b. a person sent out as an agent, often secret

c. a person who tells or announces the news

d. a person who sees or observes

37 spect, spec, spic

37.1 Meaning: to see, watch, look at

EXERCISE A Definitions of Useful spect Words

spectrum Newton proved that white light is actually composed of all the colors of the spectrum.

retrospect The summer days of our childhood seem calm, almost dull, in retrospect, but at the time, each day was exciting, full of adventure and new experiences.

despicable Is there anything more despicable than cruelty to a child?

perspective A person who is at the center of a family conflict loses his or her sense of perspective.

aspect One good aspect of the world's energy problem is that people are aware of it.

specimen Serious butterfly collectors will spend great amounts of time and effort to add a new specimen to their collection.

1.____________ A state or phrase in which something appears or may be looked at

2.____________ A review or a looking back at the past

3.____________ A sample; one out of many to show what all are like (something to be looked at)

4.____________ The range of radiant energies according to their wave length; the part of this range that we can see goes from red to violet

5.____________ Regarded or looked at with scorn or contempt

6.____________ A way of looking at things or events to judge their relative importance

38 graph, gram

38.1 Meaning: to write

EXERCISE A Definitions of Useful graph Words

graph A graph showing comparative population growth in two countries is easier to understand than pages of explanation and statistics.

epigram Few people know the author of this epigram: The greatest of faults is to be conscious of none.

diagram This diagram clearly shows the difference in wing structure in the pigeon and the eagle.

photographer Most photographers prefer to use black and white film for architectural subjects.

monograph He wanted to write a monograph on the great painter Vermeer.

graphic A graphic description of a stomach operation is not welcome at the dinner table.

1.____________ A short book or booklet written about a single thing or person

2.____________ A chart that shows a set of interrelationships, sometimes by the usc of dots or upright bars

3.____________ A bright or amusing thought expressed cleverly in a few words

4.____________ One who takes pictures with a camera (one who writes with light)

5.____________ Described clearly and with vivid details

6.____________ A line drawing, as for scientific purposes

39 mot, mob, mo

39.1 Meaning: to move, set in motion

EXERCISE A Definitions of Useful mot Words

motive	Detectives trying to solve a murder case look for a person with a motive and an opportunity.
emotion	Which is the stronger emotion: love or hate?
mobile	Americans are increasingly mobile, to the extent that less than half of them die in the town or city in which they were born.
remote	Because of great advances in transportation and communication, it is becoming difficult to find a truly remote village, where life is untouched by modern civilization.

momentum A heavy object rolling down the side of a hill picks up tremendous momentum by the time it reaches the bottom.

demote When two companies merge to form one company, some managers lose their jobs and others are demoted.

1.____________ Characterized by moving or by ease of movement; not stationary or fixed

2.____________ The opposite of promote; to move some-one into a lower classification

3.____________ A feeling or state such as joy or anger (in other words, one's feelings are moved)

4.____________ Something within individuals that causes them to do something (something that moves them)

5.____________ The power and intensity of the force of movement

6.____________ At a great distance, so as to be out of the way or apart (moved far away)

40 cred, credit

40.1 Meaning: to believe, put trust in

EXERCISE A Definitions of Useful cred Words

incredible Susan's story was incredible, but since she never lied or even exaggerated, they believed her.

credit We seem to find it easier to criticize people for their mistakes than to give them credit for the good that they have done.

incredulous When George finished telling the story of the accident, one look at the incredulous faces of his listeners made him realize that they did not believe him.

creed It is against the sporting person's creed to take unfair advantage of an opponent.

discreditable Mr. Smith was not promoted to the position of president of the company because

	of his discreditable personal behavior.
accredited	At an accredited university, graduate courses are usually taught only by persons with a Ph.D. degree.

1.____________	Honor given to a person for work done; recognition of effort or work
2.____________	Showing disbelief
3.____________	Disgraceful, dishonorable
4.____________	Certified or authorized as being of a certain desirable standard (can be trusted to be at that level)
5.____________	A summary of principles or opinions held by a person (a set of ideas that are believed)
6.____________	Too extraordinary or unusual to be believed

REVIEW OF SECTIONS 37, 38, 39, and 40

EXERCISE A Recall of Useful Words

spect, spec, spic [Section 37]

1.____________ The state in which something appears or may be looked at [a-----]

2.____________ A review or looking back at the past [--tro-----]

3.____________ A sample [----im--]

4.____________ The range of colors [-----ru-]

5.____________ Regarded with scorn [de----able]

6.____________ A way of looking at things or events to judge their relative importance [pe------ive]

graph, gram [Section 38]

1.____________ A book about a particular subject [mo-------]

2.____________ A chart showing a set of interrelationships, sometimes by the use of dots connected with lines [-----]

3.____________ A bright thought expressed in a few witty words [e-----m]

4.____________ One who takes pictures with a camera [--oto-----er]

5.____________ Described clearly and vividly [-----ic]

6.____________ A line grawing, usually for explanatory purposes [d-----m]

mot, mob, mo [Section 39]

1.____________ Characterized by ease of movement; not stationary [---ile]

2.____________ The opposite of promote [------]

3.____________ A strong feeling, such as joy or anger [e-----n]

4.____________ Something within a person which causes him or her to do something [---ive]

5.____________ The power or force of a moving body [--men---]

6.____________ Out of the way, very far away [r----e]

cred, credit [Section 40]

1.____________ Honor that is given to a person for something done [------]

2.____________ Showing disbelief [------ulous]

3.____________ Disgraceful, dishonorable [d--------able]

4.____________ Certified as being of a certain standard [ac------ed]

5.____________ Too improbable to be believed [in-----ble]

6.____________ Principles held by a person [----d]

EXERCISE B Recall of Useful Words

1. What a________ of life in modern Japan interests you most?
2. The editor of the magazine asked the author to prepare a dia________ so that the average reader could understand his article better.
3. A ________ile home is a trailer, rather like a large box on wheels, with kitchen, bathroom, and sleeping facilities, which can be pulled by a car or a special truck.
4. His e________tion was so great that tears came to his eyes.

5. A state teacher's license must be held by all who teach at an ac________ed school in California.
6. Infrared rays are beyond the red end of the visible _______rum.
7. It is in________ible that a person of eighty can swim the English Channel.
8. In this ________, you can see that for the past thirty years, the death rare has been lower than the birth rate.
9. When the explorers pushed their way through the jungle and came at last to are________e village, they were amazed to find old Coca-Cola bottles.
10. When Mary was a patient in the hospital, she felt that the nurses did all the work while the doctors took all the ________.
11. This mineral ________imen looks like rock that contains gold, but it is worthless.
12. Some teenagers feel that their lives consist of equal parts of suffering and embarrassment, but as adults, they see this period of their lives in retro________as carefree and happy.
13. Her death was so unexpected that they were in_______ulous when they first heard the news.

14. Mary is a great conversationalist, always ready with a joke or an epi________.
15. The photo________er had a difficult task trying to take a picture of the active baby.
16. George received a salary cut when he was de________ed.
17. What was the ________ive for this horrible crime?
18. Susan's personal ________calls for absolute and complete truthfulness in any and every situation.
19. From the per________ive of an adult, the actions of a teenager may be difficult to understand.
20. The students were thrilled to meet the author of the famous mono________ which they had studied so carefully.
21. All teachers see cheating as a dis________able act, but a few students regard it as mutual aid, or helpfulness.
22. Once the project got started, it seemed to move ahead under its own ________mentum, without any work on the part of the director and his assistants.
23. You are completely de________able! she shouted angrily.
24. She never finished reading the book because of the author's ________ic description of the torture of political prisoners.

EXERCISE C Using the Meanings of Roots to Understand Words

1. He gave the president his *credentials.*
   a. documents written by himself
   b. letters asking for money
   c. papers showing that someone can be trusted
   d. any papers placed before an important person

2. There are many *typographical* errors in the book.
   a. spelling
   b. printing
   c. factual
   d. grammatical

3. Few people need to use a *barograph.*
   a. an instrument which draws in air and pushes it out
   b. an instrument used to see distant objects
   c. an instrument used to move small quantities of metal along a narrow pipe
   d. an instrument that measures atmospheric pressure and records it on paper

4. There were many *spectators* at the football game.
   a. onlookers, people who watch
   b. journalists, people who write for newspapers
   c. gamblers, people who bet money
   d. hawkers, people who move through a crowd selling things

5. That story is now *discredited.*
   a. not believed
   b. not heard
   c. not told
   d. not written

6. She is extremely *circumspect.*
   a. bold, moving or rushing anywhere without regard for the consequences
   b. confident, with a sincere belief that she is right
   c. careful, looking at or examining all possible consequences
   d. changeable, folding or bending according to circumstances

7. In the art museum, John saw a lovely *mobile.*
   a. a painting made by using special way of writing with oil paint
   b. a work of art that is made of colored glass, to be shown in a window with the light behind it
   c. a painting made by throwing paintbrushes at a wall until a picture is formed
   d. a work of art made of pieces or parts that move when air moves past

8. A bullfight is an exciting *spectacle.*
   a. an event that cannot be believed
   b. a public scene which attracts the eye by its color, size, etc.
   c. a public happening which moves from one part of the city to another
   d. an event that can be written about in any language

9. When danger is near, some animals protect themselves by *immobility.*
   a. diminishing or decreasing in size
   b. changing their coloration so that they cannot be seen
   c. remaining motionless, not moving
   d. throwing themselves into any nearby hole

10. They read a book about *ideograms.*

a. great ideas that have come down to us from olden times

b. pictures used as a way to write, as in early Egyptian hieroglyphs

c. theories that we can believe, because scientific evidence proves them

d. facts that have been collected or put together by scientists

41 duc, duct

41.1 Meaning: to lead

EXERCISE A Definitions of Useful duc Words

conduct	It is a proud day when a young couple first conduct friends and relatives on a tour of their new home.
reduce	Some airline companies reduce the price of their tickets for students.
conducivc	To be conducive to study, a room should be quiet and well lit.
seduce	Seduced by promises of money and favors, people may betray their country.
deduction	Deductions for social security and income tax are made before the wage earner receives a paycheck.
duct	Water from the tear ducts keeps the surface of the eyeball moist and free of dust.

1.____________ Subtraction, the act of taking away; the part that is subtracted or taken away

2.____________ To lead

3.____________ Helpful, contributive (leading towards)

4.____________ A tube or canal that carries something, usually fluids (a thing that leads liquids from one place to another)

5.____________ To lessen, make smaller (to lead down)

6.____________ To lead someone to do something morally wrong

42 stat, sta, stit, sist

42.1 Meaning: to stand, cause to stand

EXERCISE A Definitions of Useful stat Words

consistent	Psychologists declare that it does not matter whether parents are permissive or strict, so long as they are consistent.
substantial	A substantial rise in prices will bring protests from buyers.
status	A promotion is sometimes welcomed not because of a higher salary, but because of higher status.
constitute	The parents and their children constitute what sociologists call the nuclear family.
estate	It is common practice for a man's estate, upon his death, to be divided among his children.

stabilize	In extreme situations, the government may need to take steps to stabilize prices and wages.

1.____________	To form, to make up
2.____________	A person's property in land and buildings, or more loosely, one's fortune and possessions
3.____________	Unchanging, uniform, the same (standing, not moving)
4.____________	To keep something from changing; that is, to act to hold it steady (to cause it to stand rather than to move)
5.____________	Considerable, large
6.____________	Rank, position, standing

43 tend, tens, tent

43.1 Meaning: to stretch, weaken

EXERCISE A Definitions of Useful tend Words

intense Intense grief or sorrow may cause physical problems such as loss of weight.

contend At the trial, the lawyer contended that her client was innocent because he had no motive for the crime.

extent To what extent is an individual responsible for his or her actions?

intensive An intensive language-learning program may call for twenty-five to forty hours per week in the classroom.

tension A psychologist can see by the way a person sits and speaks whether that person is suffering from nervous tension.

pretense	Under the pretense of going to the toilet, George left the classroom and slipped out the side gate of the school.
1.____________	Concentrated (everything stretched towards one purpose)
2.____________	Space or amount to which something reaches (stretches); therefore: degree, amount, size, length, etc.
3.____________	To an extreme degree, great (stretched to the utmost)
4.____________	Strain (being stretched out rather than relaxed)
5.____________	Excuse (something falsely stretched out as true in order to deceive someone)
6.____________	To argue, assert

44 fer, lat

44.1 Meaning: to carry, bear

EXERCISE A Definitions of Useful fer (lat) Words

elation	A teenager's mood swings from depression to elation and back again with surprising frequency.
infer	We may infer from a person's unusual silence that he or she is angry or upset.
fertile	Fertile soil and abundant rain are what a farmer wants.
confer	A businessperson sometimes confers with a lawyer before signing an important contract.
differentiate	The law courts differentiate between murder committed in the heat of passion and murder coldly planned in advance.

deference	In most cultures, the wealthy are treated with deference.

1.____________ To consult, compare views

2.____________ To discriminate, to recognize the difference between two things

3.____________ Extreme joy or happiness (being lifted or carried up emotionally)

4.____________ Productive, producing in abundance, as a tree produces or bears fruit

5.____________ To draw a conclusion from the facts by reasoning; to understand what is indirectly stated

6.____________ Courteous or polite regard for another person's wishes

A VOCABULARY WORKBOOK THRU READING

REVIEW OF SECTIONS 41, 42, 43, and 44

EXERCISE A Recall of Useful Words

duc, duct [Section 41]

1.__________ Subtraction, the act of taking away; the part that is taken away [de------n]

2.__________ To lead [c-----t]

3.__________ Helpful, contributive [c-----ive]

4.__________ A tube or canal that carries something, usually a fluid [----]

5.__________ To lessen, make smaller [re----]

6.__________ To lead someone to do something evil [s----e]

stat, sta, stit, sist [Section 42]

1.__________ To form, to make up [con-----te]

2.__________ Land and property owned by a person [e----e]

3.____________ Uniform, unchanging [c------ent]

4.____________ To keep something from changing [------ize]

5.____________ Considerable [sub------al]

6.____________ Position or rank [----us]

tend, tens, tent [Section 43]

1.____________ Concentrated [in-----ve]

2.____________ Degree, amount, length, etc. [ex----]

3.____________ To an extreme degree [in-----]

4.____________ Strain, the opposite of relaxation [----ion]

5.____________ Excuse [pr-----e]

6.____________ To argue, put forth an argument [c-----d]

fer, lat [Section 44]

1.____________ To consult; to hold a conference [c-----]

2.____________ To discriminate [d-------tiate]

3.____________ Extreme joy or happiness [e-----n]

4.____________ Productive [----ile]

5.____________ To draw a conclusion from what is done or indirectly stated by a person [i----]

6.____________ Courteous regard for another person's wishes [d------ce]

EXERCISE B Recall of Useful Words

1. A young person's mind is _______tile ground for new ideas and theories.
2. Children feel the _______ion between unhappy, quarreling parents.
3. Her died childless, so his huge e_______e was inherited by a nephew.
4. A criminal's actions con_______ute a threat to society.
5. Should we in_______ from your silence that you agree to our plan? they asked.
6. After the workload was re_______ed, the employees were satisfied.
7. In this new apartment, _______s for the electric wiring are hidden by beautiful wood panels.
8. They immediately saw through his pre_______e that he was a Spanish prince and notified the police.
9. They were unable to determine the ex_______ of the damage until some time after the earthquake.
10. He expressed his e_______ion over the birth of his first child by giving cigars to all his friends.

11. Thanks to good medical care, there was a sub_______ntial improvement in Susan's health after a few days.
12. During the last two months of the final year of secondary school, many students follow an in_______ive study program.
13. A younger person's de_______ence to an older person is expected in many cultures.
14. Se_______ed by her youth and beauty, he left his wife and children.
15. The teacher's obvious interest in the students' ideas, and the relaxed atmosphere in the classroom, were con_______ive to lively discussions in which all participated.
16. The composition was extremely well written, except that the quality of the third paragraph was not con_______tent with that of the other paragraph.
17. The lawyer for both parties stepped forward in court to con_______ privately with the judge.
18. In calculating your income tax, you are allowed to make a de_______ion for medical expenses.
19. Her in_______e interest in ancient Rome motivated her to travel to Italy.

20. Because of his new ________us as bank president, Mr. Jones sold his Volkswagen and bought a Mercedes.
21. In some countries, following a divorce, ex-husbands con________ that wealthy ex-wives should pay them alimony (money for support).
22. They decided to postpone any action until economic and political conditions were ________bilized.
23. Should an employer dif________entiate between men and women employees in the matter of salaries?
24. Important visitors from the Department of Health were con________ed around the hospital by the director herself.

EXERCISE C Using the Meanings of Roots to Understand Words

1. An electrical machine is often made up of a *stator* and a rotor.

   a. a part that is fixed or stands still

   b. a part that moves around another part

   c. a part that holds many other parts

   d. a part that can repair itself if it is broken

2. When John graduated from the university, he kept up a *tenuous* relationship with his old friends.
   a. fixed
   b. full of trust
   c. with his mind, not his heart
   d. weak

3. The doctor recommended *ablation* of the diseased kidney.
   a. external treatment, applying heat or chemicals to the skin in the region near the kidney
   b. cutting, opening the body to examine the kidney
   c. internal treatment, introducing medicine directly into the kidney
   d. carrying away, removal of the kidney

4. After eating so much, John had a feeling of *distension.*
   a. being unable to move
   b. being stretched or swollen
   c. being extremely thirsty
   d. being folded or bent

5. In parts of the Sahara desert, *aquifers* lie deep below the surface.
   a. layers of rock that hold or bear water
   b. unchanging, fixed layers of rock
   c. layers of rock that are slowly moving as the centuries pass
   d. layers of rock that cannot be seen

6. Mary's best quality is that she is *persistent.*
   a. bearing knowledge, able to recall and state many facts and figures
   b. leading others, serving as a good example to her fellow workers
   c. stretching her mind, eager to learn about new ideas and theories
   d. standing firm, in spite of difficulties, warnings, etc.

7. That year Susan noticed an *attenuation* of her physical strength.
   a. strengthening or increase
   b. variation or change
   c. weakening or lessening
   d. steadiness or lack of change

8. Gold is a *ductile* metal.

   a. bears or has great value

   b. can be led or drawn out and hammered thin

   c. holds or keeps its shape

   d. can take other metals to form a mixture called an alloy

9. Because of his fright, John was *stationary.*

   a. moving, or running, very rapidly

   b. weakened by fear

   c. not moving, standing still

   d. shouting for help

10. We all know the meaning of the word *education* as it is used today. We should remember the original meaning, too, of the prefix **ex** and the root **duc.**

    a. to put in or add to the facts stored in a child's brain

    b. to stretch the brain so that it will hold more facts

    c. to move the child so that he or she is willing to take in many facts

    d. to draw forth or lead out what is within the child

저자약력

노이균

KBS 제1라디오 '노이균의 생활영어' 진행
고려대학교에서 영문학(영시) 전공
The University of Edinburgh에서 영문학(영시) 전공
The University of California, Los Angeles에서 TESL(Teaching English as a Second Language) 전공

A Vocabulary Workbook Thru Reading

2018년 8월 10일 초판 1쇄 인쇄
2018년 8월 15일 초판 1쇄 발행

지은이 노이균
펴낸이 진욱상
펴낸곳 (주)백산출판사
교 정 편집부
본문디자인 구효숙
표지디자인 오정은

저자와의 합의하에 인지첩부 생략

등 록 2017년 5월 29일 제406-2017-000058호
주 소 경기도 파주시 회동길 370(백산빌딩 3층)
전 화 02-914-1621(代)
팩 스 031-955-9911
이메일 edit@ibaeksan.kr
홈페이지 www.ibaeksan.kr

ISBN 979-11-88892-72-3 03740
값 15,000원